# London's Underground

# London's Underground

## The Story of the Tube

**Oliver Green**

Photographs by Benjamin Graham

WHITE
LION
PUBLISHING

PREVIOUS PAGE: A Tube train reflected in the platform tiling at Marble Arch station on the Central line, 2018. This is on the original Twopenny Tube, opened in 1900 and fully refurbished in the 1980s.

OPPOSITE: Station subway entrance at Oxford Circus, 2018, clearly flagged by the Underground roundel. The Tube logo, now more than a century old, not only signifies a station, but has become a symbol of London itself which is recognised internationally.

# Introduction

OPPOSITE: Green Park became the first deep Tube station in central London to have unrestricted street-to-train access in 2011. Beyond these steps on the south side of Piccadilly is a ramped entrance from the park and lift access from the street to the booking hall from an elegant Portland stone lift canopy designed by Acanthus Architects. The entrance building incorporates *Sea Strata*, fossil carvings commissioned by Art on the Underground from artist John Maine. It was all completed for the 2012 London Olympics and Paralympics, a great recent example of stylish and practical applied art and design on London Underground.

The London Underground, now popularly known as the Tube, has its origins in the Metropolitan Railway, which opened in January 1863. It was the original urban metro, the first passenger-carrying underground railway in the world. The Metropolitan Railway originally used steam locomotives to pull gas-lit wooden carriages over a 6 km (3.75 miles) sub-surface route between Paddington and Farringdon, now part of London Underground's Circle, Hammersmith & City and Metropolitan lines. Much of the hardy Victorian infrastructure survives in everyday use.

Construction of this original line took less than three years and the working railway proved an immediate success with passengers. In the first year of operation, 9.5 million journeys were made on this short subterranean railway. *The Times* newspaper, which had referred to the Metropolitan Railway sceptically as a 'bold but hazardous proposition', was soon referring to it as 'the great engineering triumph of the day'.

London was then the greatest city in the world, with a rapidly growing population of more than 3 million people. Travelling up to the metropolis from every part of the country had been revolutionized over the previous twenty-five years. The capital already had nine main-line termini for trains arriving from every direction, and more were planned. However, most of the stations were some distance from the city centre and they were not connected.

The Metropolitan Railway was a novel attempt to solve a slightly different transport problem: how to get around or across the congested city quickly and conveniently. At the Parliamentary Select Committee on Metropolitan Communications in 1855, one witness who gave evidence complained that it took longer to get across town, navigating the crowded streets from London Bridge to Paddington, than it did to travel up to London by train from Brighton.

Some might argue that the situation has not improved much, but the growth and development of London's underground railway system over more than 150 years have been phenomenal, and it is now impossible to imagine life in the city without access to its rapid transit below the surface. From the original seven stations, the London Underground has expanded to serve 270 stations across Greater London and is closely integrated with other rail-based modes of transport in the city region, complementing the Docklands Light Railway, London Trams, London Overground, Crossrail (the Elizabeth line) and a vast network of suburban rail lines.

Today, there are eleven electric Underground lines, each identified by their own colour on the official Tube map. The tracks cover 402 km (250 miles), thus making London Underground the third longest metro system in the world and the largest in Europe. In the twenty-first century, the network carries record numbers of passengers, with up to

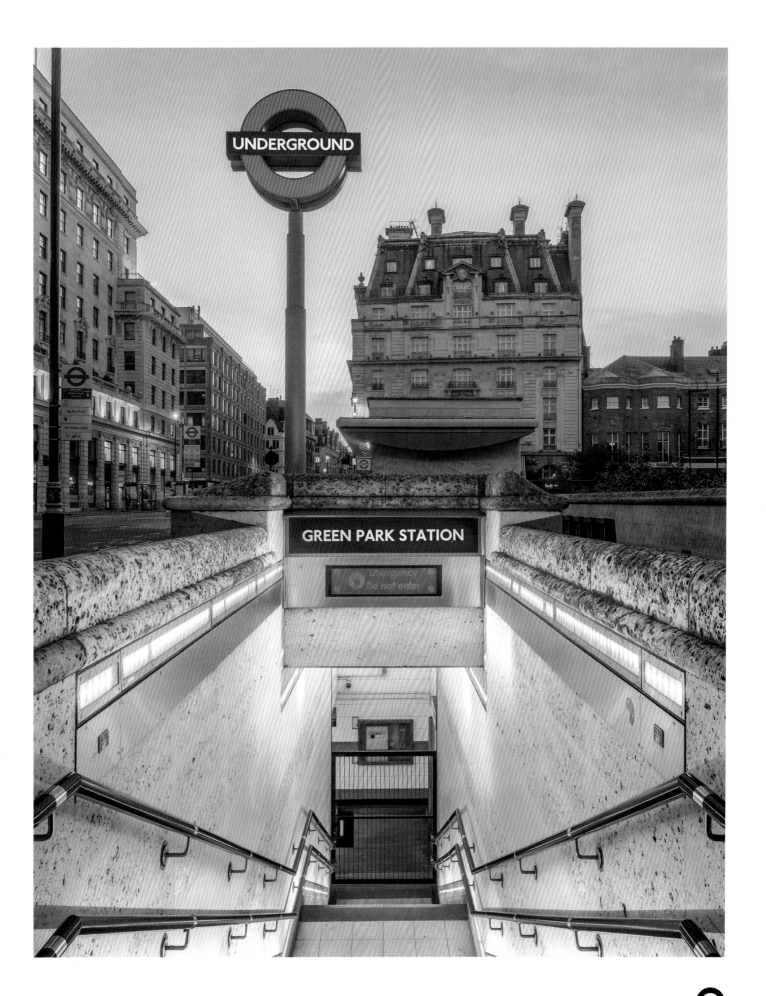

1.4 billion passenger journeys made each year, more than the total for the entire national rail network.

The population of Greater London has increased to more than 8 million, and the use of the Underground system has grown rapidly too, as more people travel greater distances into London to work, for leisure or to visit from overseas. London is now a world city, an international metropolis that everyone wants to experience, and nearly all of those travellers use the Tube as part of their journey.

It is no exaggeration to describe the Underground as the lifeblood of the city. Over a period of more than 150 years, its look, design and engineering have become a unique part of London's character. As the system developed, steam trains gave way to electric power, deep Tubes succeeded shallow covered cuttings, and lifts and escalators were installed for vertical transit – all innovations that we now take for granted. Before long, the Tube had its own distinctive typeface, devised

in 1916 by calligrapher Edward Johnston, who also developed the famous bar-and-circle symbol. Later, in 1933, came Harry Beck's brilliant diagrammatic map, based on electrical circuit diagrams, which wildly distorted London's geography but made Underground travel far less daunting. Even seventy-five years ago, this carefully devised travel aid made using the Tube simple and straightforward in a way that the New York Subway and the Paris Métro are not.

Between the wars, a complete corporate identity and a consistent design style – covering everything from trains and station environments to communication systems – evolved, led by London Underground's inspired managing director Frank Pick and consulting architect Charles Holden. Their distinctive 'London look', which became unique to the Tube in the 1930s, was further developed and adapted in the post-war years, although innovation and spending were constrained by austerity. New technology was applied sparingly, for example

on the computer-controlled Victoria line in 1968 and later with the high-tech design style of the Jubilee line extension in 1999. All this makes the twenty-first-century Underground and its characterful, changing environment far more than a basic urban transit system. It represents and serves London in so many ways and has its own image and style; city life without it is almost unimaginable.

The evolution of the London Underground has often been inconsistent and even haphazard, as has the city's own development. Different political and financial pressures, changing economic circumstances, war and austerity, and a management culture ranging from ambition to neglect have made it a bumpy ride. The need to improve the Underground environment and the capacity of the Tube will always be a challenge as the capital moves on.

A fascinating characteristic of London's Underground is its ability to showcase a rich and unique 150-year heritage within a progressive metro system, which continues to grow and modernize without destroying or discarding its past. Travelling on the Tube is like a journey through a complex archaeological time trail, fascinating but often frustrating, and difficult to explain and untangle.

This book combines a guide to London Underground's history and evolution with a photographer's view of the system today. It is not always a comfortable journey, but sometimes it is worth stopping to admire what has been achieved rather than rushing through the crowd. The Tube always has been, and still is, quite a triumph.

BELOW: 150 years of history at Gloucester Road. The Victorian station was given heritage listed status and extensively renovated in the 1980s. Art on the Underground now curates changing exhibitions along the disused platform here, seen in the background, which runs alongside the original arched retaining wall of 1868.

# Steam Underground

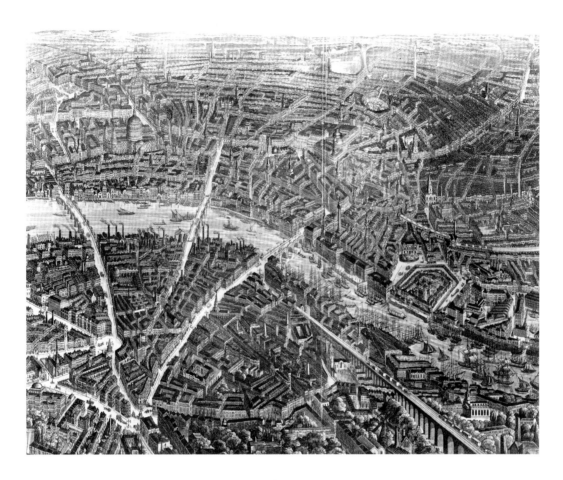

## A London Pioneer

Proposals to build the world's first underground railway came out of the search for a solution to London's growing traffic problems and the congestion on its streets. By the mid-nineteenth century, Britain's capital was the largest and most prosperous city in the world. Its success as a port and commercial centre, based on Britain's rapidly growing empire, led to an unprecedented explosion in the city's population.

This rose from just under 1 million at the first census in 1801 to more than 2.5 million fifty years later, when the Great Exhibition of 1851 provided London's first major tourist attraction in Joseph Paxton's Crystal Palace. Most of the many thousands of visitors from out of town, whether from elsewhere in Britain or from overseas, arrived in London at a main-line station and then had to walk or fight for a seat on an omnibus in order to reach Hyde Park. There were no railways across the capital, and only the Great Western Railway (GWR) terminus at Paddington, through which visitors from the west of England arrived, was close to the park.

The unprecedented crowds that thronged to the Great Exhibition highlighted for the first time a pressing issue of which Londoners and regular visitors were well aware. Improved communications and transport within and across the metropolis were becoming essential to unlock the impossible congestion on the city's main thoroughfares, where people,

horses, carts, wagons, cabs, omnibuses and livestock being driven to market could bring the streets to a virtual standstill.

The first main-line railways established separate London termini at London Bridge (1836), Euston (1837), Paddington (1838), Shoreditch (1840) and Fenchurch Street (1841). There were many more railway promotions in the 'railway mania' of the 1840s, when the House of Commons had to consider 435 railway bills for England and Wales. These were all private enterprise schemes in which the government had no direct involvement, but every project had to be scrutinized and authorized by Parliament. This 'light touch' state regulation was standard procedure in Victorian Britain and could both delay and frustrate major infrastructure projects. A Royal Commission on London termini was established in 1846 to consider the particular problem of railways entering the City and Westminster, and immediately answered its own question by defining a central railway-free zone. At this stage, only one small terminus, Fenchurch Street, had opened within the 'square mile' of the City of London and none of the lines from the south had bridged the river. Even so, the existing railways on the edge of London were contributing to the congestion at the centre, and rail companies without a direct connection to the business centre were pushing to get access for themselves. Eventually, the number of rail termini in London rose to fifteen by the end of the nineteenth century, more than any other city in the world. The idea of a single, giant *Hauptbahnhof* (central station) to accommodate all main lines to a city, as later developed in Germany, was never seriously considered for London and would probably never have been agreed between the competing private railway companies.

However, back in the 1840s and 1850s, both Parliament and the City Corporation were determined to keep central London free of railways and, as one historian neatly put it, 'hold back the London termini at an invisible ring wall'. This ruling was not an absolute embargo but it was a strong recommendation to Select Committees considering future railway bills. In fact, promoters were already discouraged by the high costs of acquiring land and demolishing property, and by the actions taken by the landed aristocracy to preserve the integrity of their central London estates. In 1855, another Parliamentary Select Committee on Metropolitan Communications recommended, as a potential solution, that the existing and future main-line termini in London should be linked by an underground railway, but offered no detail as to how this might be achieved.

The idea was not new, having first been suggested in the 1830s. One of its earliest advocates was the City Corporation's solicitor Charles Pearson. He was an unusually forward-thinking man who could see both economic and social benefits to linking the main-line railways with the City.

Pearson proposed a railway with up to eight tracks running in a covered way under a broad new road down the Fleet valley from King's Cross to a large goods and passenger terminal at Farringdon. This was to form part of an existing improvement scheme to clear the insanitary slum areas of Clerkenwell. The displaced inhabitants, Pearson suggested, could move out to healthier suburbs and be offered cheap fares for a daily train journey to work in the centre of town.

It was an appealing but idealistic vision that not surprisingly failed to attract investors, although cheap workmen's fares were later put in place by Parliament as a way to force railway companies to provide some social compensation for their urban projects. The City Terminus Company was formed in 1852 to pursue Pearson's scheme, but neither the City Corporation nor the main-line companies showed any enthusiasm for funding it.

A separate, more commercially motivated underground venture, originally known as the Bayswater, Paddington & Holborn Bridge Railway, was proposed at this time. Unlike Pearson's scheme, this did not involve expensive property demolition or costly road building, but would be routed mainly below the New Road between King's Cross and Paddington, running very close to a third main-line station at Euston on the way. John Hargreaves Stevens, one of Pearson's colleagues, was appointed surveyor, with the experienced

ABOVE: 'London Bridge Traffic'. from an article in the *Illustrated London News*, 1859, commenting on the growing traffic congestion in the City of London and the proposed Metropolitan Railway scheme to combat it.

LEFT: Charles Pearson, the City Corporation's solicitor, c.1860.

OPPOSITE, ABOVE: London Bridge station had no shelter or passenger facilities on the viaduct when it first opened in 1836.

OPPOSITE, BELOW: Euston station, terminus of the London and Birmingham Railway (L&BR), 1837. This was the first main line to London. At first, trains were hauled up Camden Bank by cable and steam locomotives were attached at the top.

LEFT: John Fowler, engineer of the Metropolitan and District Railways.

ABOVE: 'Proposed station at Baker Street' from the *Illustrated London News*, 7 April 1860.

BELOW: Farringdon station today, as rebuilt at street level in 1923 to the design of Met architect Charles W. Clark. It was then known as Farringdon & High Holborn station.

OPPOSITE: Cut-and-cover construction of the Metropolitan at King's Cross, 1861, looking west. The tower of the Great Northern Railway's main-line terminus, opened in 1852, is in the centre. St Pancras station and hotel were built next door by the Midland Railway in the late 1860s.

John (later Sir John) Fowler as engineer. In many respects, this line was the true originator of the London Underground, and while Pearson's grander and more altruistic plan failed, the rival scheme received royal assent in 1853 as the North Metropolitan Railway. The two projects were then effectively merged so that crucial access to the City could be secured, and a firm final project, renamed the Metropolitan Railway, gained parliamentary approval in 1854.

Money was still a problem though, and even with the King's Cross to Farringdon section scaled down to a modest double-track railway, the total capital requirement for the whole line was now put at £1 million. With a depressed money market in the late 1850s, the Metropolitan Railway was almost wound up in despair in 1858, with £1,000 of shareholder money spent on advertising in a last-ditch attempt to attract funding. Pearson's personal commitment to the project proved critical, when he at last persuaded his employer – the City Corporation – to make a financial contribution. Business in the City, he argued, was being damaged by the congested roads and workers forced to live in squalid conditions in Clerkenwell so that they could walk to work. He remained resolutely philanthropic in his vision, telling Metropolitan shareholders that 'no English railway scheme could hope to attain support unless it could be shown to be useful to the public', but adding that it must also of course be profitable for its investors. With the City's

financial support and further contributions secured from the GWR and the Great Northern Railway (GNR), which would both have running rights over the Metropolitan, enough capital was at last forthcoming to allow construction to begin in 1860.

**Creating the Metropolitan**

The original contracts specified that the railway should be completed in twenty-one months, but, in the way that has become familiar with large infrastructure projects ever since, work fell behind schedule. Eventually, a well-publicized trial journey over the whole line took place on 24 May 1862. Chief engineer Fowler was present and the guests included William Gladstone, then Chancellor of the Exchequer, who was also a shareholder. It was announced with confidence that the railway would open to the public in July, but on 18 June disaster struck. The Fleet River, which had been diverted into a brick sewer alongside the railway, burst through the retaining walls near Farringdon Street and flooded the line to a depth of 3 m (10 ft) as far back as King's Cross. Fortunately, nobody was injured, but the damage took six weeks to repair. Further delay was caused by the government inspector's insistence on changes to the block signalling system before public traffic could be allowed.

At last, a formal opening ceremony took place on 9 January 1863, with a trip along the line for guests followed by a banquet at Farringdon Street station. The following day, Saturday

Paddington (District and Circle) station was on the first section of the Metropolitan's extension through Bayswater, which opened in 1868 and was originally called Praed Street. At platform level it is still in its original condition as a brick-lined cutting with an overall roof (see page 29).

## Cut and Cover

Two separate contracts for the underground railway were awarded in December 1859, and the first shafts were sunk at King's Cross and near Euston Square in February 1860. Most of the line west of King's Cross was built directly below the New Road (now the Marylebone and Euston Roads) using the 'cut-and-cover' method to create a covered trench housing the railway rather than a true tunnel. It avoided the cost and risk of property demolition but led to months of disruption. The section between King's Cross and Farringdon was built partly in an open cutting but included the only true tunnel on the line, running for nearly half a mile under the hill of Mount Pleasant in Clerkenwell, which at its deepest was nearly 18 m (60 ft) below ground level.

The basic cut-and-cover approach appeared simple enough, employing existing technology to build the railway within an excavated cutting. The innovation lay in covering the cutting with a tunnel roof and a relaid main road above it that could take the weight of London's traffic while ensuring a properly ventilated environment below. Journalist Henry Mayhew wrote in 1865:

Learned engineers were not wanting to foretell how the projected tunnel must necessarily fall in from the mere weight of the traffic in the streets above, and how the adjacent houses would not only be shaken to their foundations by the vibrations of the engines, but the families residing in them would be one and all poisoned by the sulphurous exhalations from the fuel with which the boilers were heated.

Fowler and his expert engineering colleagues, including Isambard Kingdom Brunel, had been surprisingly dismissive of these concerns when first making the case for an underground railway to a parliamentary committee in 1854. Ventilation, in particular, was loftily brushed aside by Brunel. 'I thought', he told the committee, 'the impression had been exploded long since that railway tunnels required much ventilation.' The railway was approved and it was only when operation began nine years later that some of the inadequacies of the infrastructure were revealed.

In *Our Iron Roads*, a popular account of railway development published in 1885, Frederick S. Williams describes the apparent chaos of construction from the point of view of exasperated local residents:

> The exact operation could be but dimly seen or heard from the street by the curious observer who gazed between the tall boards that shut him out; but paterfamilias, from his house hard by, could look down on an infinite chaos of timber, shaft holes, ascending and descending chains and iron buckets which brought rubbish from below to be carted away; or perhaps one morning he found workmen had been kindly shoring up his family abode with huge timbers to make it safer.
>
> . . . he can hardly get out to business or home to supper without slipping, and he strongly objects to a temporary way of wet planks, erected for his use and the use of passers-by, over a yawning cavern under the pavement.

**LEFT: King's Cross Metropolitan Railway station under construction in 1862 and as opened in 1863, with broad-gauge GWR trains. The present Metropolitan and Circle line station at King's Cross lies further west and opened in 1941.**

10 January 1863, the first urban underground railway in the world opened its station doors to the public. Despite predictions in the press that Londoners would never take to underground travel, the Metropolitan was well patronized from the start. On the first day alone, nearly 40,000 passengers undertook the eighteen-minute journey. One of them, Sir William Hardman, recorded his initial trip on the line with some enthusiasm:

> Mary Anne and I made our first trip down the 'Drain'. We walked to the Edgware Road and took first class tickets for King's Cross (6d each). We experienced no disagreeable odour beyond the smell common to tunnels. The carriages (broad gauge) hold ten persons, with divided seats, and are lighted by gas (two lights); they are also so lofty that a six-footer may stand erect with his hat on.

The line soon attracted regular users and sightseers, and in its first six months of operation it carried an average of 26,500 passengers per day. On weekdays, there was a train every fifteen minutes throughout most of the day, which increased to one every ten minutes at peak times. The Sunday service ran every twenty minutes, with a two-hour 'church break' in the morning when no trains operated.

Single fares were 6d first class, 4d second class and 3d third class, with returns for 9d, 6d and 5d respectively, still beyond the reach of many working-class Londoners. One early traveller who was outraged at the cost of his third-class ticket kept it as a souvenir with a tiny inscription on the back: 'Spent the whole day at 34 Albion Road . . . after exploring the new Ry, the fares along which are MONSTROUS.' This was despite the fact that from May 1864 the Metropolitan had responded to parliamentary pressure by offering cheap early morning workmen's return fares of 3d (later reduced to 2d), the first railway company in the country to do so. This helped establish the Underground as a mode of transport for all. Although class differentiation was retained, the Metropolitan soon found that 70 per cent of its passengers were travelling third class, with 20 per cent in second and just 10 per cent in first.

The provision of cheap workmen's tickets had always been a particular concern for Pearson, and he campaigned tirelessly. Sadly, the man who had worked for so long to get an underground railway built died in September 1862, just four months before the trains started running. He would certainly have been gratified to see that some of the gloomy press predictions about the railway's prospects, expressed during the construction period, proved groundless. Only a year prior to the opening, *The Times* had noted that many people regarded the whole scheme as one which, even if it could be accomplished, would certainly never pay, and was more like a grim fantasy:

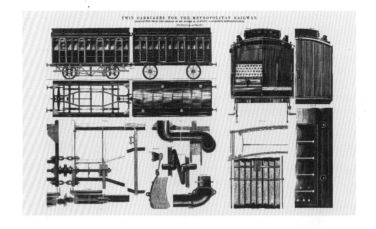

A subterranean railway under London was awfully suggestive of dark, noisome tunnels, buried many fathoms deep beyond the reach of light or life; passages inhabited by rats, soaked with sewer drippings and poisoned by the escape of gas mains. It seemed an insult to common sense to suppose that people who could travel as cheaply to the City on the outside of a Paddington bus would ever prefer, as a merely quicker medium, to be driven amid palpable darkness through the foul subsoil of London. . . . The Subterranean Railway has been talked about for years and nothing done, till the whole idea has been gradually associated with the plans for flying machines, warfare by balloons, tunnels under the Channel and other bold but somewhat hazardous propositions of the same kind.

Whatever their initial fears and misgivings, Londoners were not put off and were soon attracted underground in ever-increasing numbers. Despite the smell and the gloomy atmosphere, both compounded by inadequate ventilation, the Metropolitan quickly proved itself to be an extremely safe and efficient railway. As historian Theo Barker astutely observed: 'Had there been any bad accidents, as could well have happened in the early days of new and untried equipment, passengers would certainly have been scared away. In fact, during the whole period of steam operation, there was no fatal accident to any passenger in these cuttings and tunnels.'

When the underground railway opened, the Metropolitan did not own any rolling stock of its own. The trains were supplied by the GWR through its main-line connection at Paddington. At the time, the GWR was still operating on Brunel's broad-gauge (2,140 mm/7 ft ¼ in) track. The first section of the Metropolitan was therefore laid with dual-gauge track throughout so that standard-gauge (1,435 mm/4 ft 8½ in) trains from the GNR connection at King's Cross could also run on it. The GWR provided forty-five eight-wheeled compartment coaches, which had teak bodies and were lit by coal gas carried in inflatable weighted bags on the carriage roofs.

Motive power was initially provided by twenty-two coke-burning tank engines, designed by the GWR's locomotive engineer Daniel Gooch and built at Swindon. They were the first locomotives to be fitted with condensing apparatus for operation underground. This was a simple, although only partially successful, attempt to control emissions below ground. Steam from the cylinders was diverted into cold water tanks through large pipes on either side of the engine's boiler so as not to fill up the tunnels, but the apparatus did not control smoke from the firebox. This was still emitted from the locomotive's chimney, even when the engines used 'smokeless' coke rather than coal as fuel.

The Baker Street passenger concourse link between the Circle and Metropolitan main-line platforms, created when the station was first rebuilt in 1911. Chiltern Court was then added above in the 1920s.

WEMBLEY, HARROW,

↑ Bakerloo line
↑ Jubilee line

Metropolitan line
↑ Platforms 1 and 2
Check indicator for platform of first train

Metropol...
Platforms 3
Check indicator for platform...

Way out →

# Underground steam

The almost identical steam locomotives supplied by Beyer Peacock to both the Metropolitan and District Railways from the 1860s were used on most passenger services for forty years. Although small, they were heavy and extremely powerful, and were able to handle very effectively the short stops and rapid acceleration required from closely spaced stations. Working conditions for the driver and fireman were tough, with no cabs for weather protection, as George Spiller, a former District Railway stoker, explained in an interview many years later:

> We worked ten hour days, eight times round the Circle. In the summer you could hardly breathe going through the tunnels, it was so hot. It was enough to boil you on the footplate. I'd shovel about a ton of coal in a day's work: it was a dirty, hot, sweaty job. And there was no cover outside . . . we had to put up with rain and wind and snow.

Following electrification in 1905, most of the old steam engines were scrapped or sold on to provincial goods railways or collieries. A few remained in service on the Underground until the 1930s, mainly for shunting work or hauling trains on the Metropolitan's remote Brill branch in rural Buckinghamshire. One of these, number 23, was saved for preservation and is now on display at the London Transport Museum in Covent Garden. Stoker Spiller, who became a motorman on the new Bakerloo Tube in the 1900s, was in his nineties when he visited the museum in 1986 and recorded his memories. Despite the harsh start to his working life, he lived to celebrate his centenary.

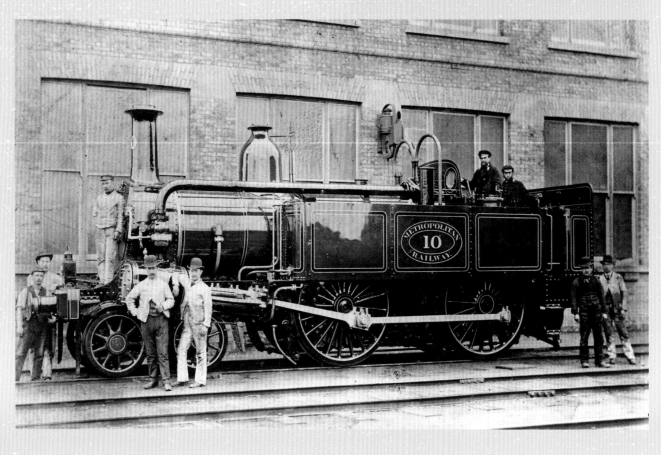

LEFT AND OPPOSITE, ABOVE: Inner Circle headboard and condensing apparatus on the Met 23 in the London Transport Museum. This is the only survivor of the original Beyer Peacock locomotive fleet built in the 1860s.

ABOVE: One of the District Railway's very similar Beyer Peacock locomotives with operating staff at Earl's Court station, c.1875.

OPPOSITE, BELOW: Metropolitan A class tank engine No. 10 outside the locomotive shed at Edgware Road, c.1880.

Fowler had originally intended to solve the problem of smoke emission in the tunnels by using a 'hot brick' locomotive. It was to have a small firebox in which to heat up a chamber of fire bricks while running on an open section of the line. Once underground, the fire would be damped down while the hot bricks continued to provide heat for the boiler without smoke. A prototype was built by Robert Stephenson in 1861, but 'Fowler's Ghost', as it became known, was not a success and never entered passenger service. In fact, the ventilation of tunnels filled with the fumes of steam locomotives became an insoluble issue for the Metropolitan and one that the railway persistently played down. It only ended with electrification at the turn of the century.

Within a few weeks of the opening of the railway, relations between the directors at the Metropolitan and the GWR broke down over both financial and operating arrangements. As a result, the GWR withdrew all of its rolling stock and the Metropolitan had no option but to order its own, hastily arranging a temporary loan of locomotives and carriages from the GNR while its own trains were being built. The new stock was provided by locomotive manufacturer Beyer Peacock of Manchester, a powerful design of heavy tank engines with open cabs and improved condensing apparatus for underground operation. The first eighteen trains were delivered in 1864, but eventually the Metropolitan ordered sixty-six to be built.

## The District and Circle

The 1860s were boom years for railway promotion in London. The first main-line extension over the river from the south was completed to a new terminus at Victoria in 1860. Other railways got permission to cross the Thames into the City itself. Another Parliamentary Select Committee decided that the best way to minimize further incursions was to follow the Metropolitan's example and go underground. Backed by the Metropolitan's board of directors, Fowler was already planning extensions to the original line east to Moorgate and west to Hammersmith. The latter was an overground branch to be run in partnership with the GWR, which opened in 1864 despite the breakdown of the agreement on train provision. Today, this is part of the Underground's Hammersmith & City line. Another feeder line running north-west from Baker Street to Finchley Road began life in 1868 as the Metropolitan and St John's Wood Railway, later to develop into the Metropolitan's main Extension line to the country.

A plan was developed to create a full 'Inner Circle' railway for London to link up the Metropolitan at both ends, with another underground line connecting the termini of the main-line extensions that crossed the river from the south to Charing Cross (1864), Ludgate Hill (1865) and Cannon Street (1866). This was a complicated scheme that involved several separate railway companies, new links and an ambitious plan to create

a new embankment for the Thames that would enclose both the railway and a new sewage system for London, to be created by the Metropolitan Board of Works under the direction of Sir Joseph Bazalgette. The whole interconnected development, which began in the 1860s, would take twenty years to complete.

A new company, the Metropolitan District Railway (usually shortened to 'District'), was formed to build the southern part of the underground railway circuit, while the Metropolitan undertook to extend its line south-west from Paddington to South Kensington and eastwards from Farringdon through the City to Tower Hill, where the two railways would eventually meet. From the start, the two companies were intended to work very closely together, leading to eventual amalgamation. Fowler was appointed engineer for the new railway works and the Metropolitan agreed to operate all train services on the 'Inner Circle' when it opened.

The District was also built by 'cut-and-cover' construction throughout, but unlike the original section of the Metropolitan the route did not lie below a wide existing street. The section between South Kensington and Westminster, where construction began, was heavily built up. A great deal of expensive property purchase and demolition was necessary, which delayed progress on the line.

The work was nearly all carried out by hand, employing some 2,000 navvies to dig out and build the infrastructure of cuttings, tunnels and stations. The men were assisted by 200 horses, which carted away the spoil and delivered materials, but the only mechanical tools available were fifty-eight steam navvies: small mobile steam cranes deployed along the route. Large temporary kilns were put up at Earl's Court, which was then at the edge of the built-up area, to bake the 140 million bricks required to construct the cutting walls.

Even so, progress was hampered by landowners imposing unreasonable demands: Lord Harrington, for example, would not allow any ventilation shafts where the line crossed his Kensington estates. There were also unexpected engineering challenges, including the need to channel the underground Westbourne River through a substantial iron pipe and box girder over the tracks at Sloane Square station. This survived a direct hit on the station during the Blitz in 1940 and can still be seen straddling the District line platforms today.

East of Westminster, the District was planned to run as far as Blackfriars along the new Thames Embankment, which had been under construction by the Metropolitan Board of Works since 1862. Unfortunately, the District's difficulty and slowness in raising capital meant that this section of the Embankment, enclosing part of Bazalgette's main sewage system for London, was virtually complete before the District's work got under way in 1869. As a result, part of the Embankment had to be ripped up and rebuilt to accommodate the railway. Despite this delay,

ABOVE: Mansion House station, the original eastern terminus of the District Railway opened in 1876. A locomotive is being coaled and watered on the far left.

OPPOSITE: Gloucester Road station nearing completion just before the opening of the District Railway in 1868 (above), and as it appeared 150 years later (below). The Piccadilly station entrance on the left was built in 1906.

RIGHT: Praed Street, Paddington, on completion of the Metropolitan extension through Bayswater and Kensington in 1868 (above) and as it is today (below). This station, which has changed very little at platform level, is now served by District and Circle line trains only.

the remaining construction work was quite straightforward and trains were running through to Blackfriars by May 1870.

This might have seemed the logical time for the Metropolitan and District Railways to merge into a single company, but relations between the two were already at a low ebb over the operating agreement. The District did not own any locomotives or rolling stock, and in return for running all its services the Metropolitan intended to claim half the ticket receipts. This looked like a rerun of the dispute with the GWR that arose soon after the Metropolitan first opened in 1863. At the beginning of 1870, nearly six months before the trains were running, the District announced that it planned to end this arrangement and gave the required eighteen months' notice to the Metropolitan. It was a rather empty declaration of independence because the two companies would always have to cooperate somehow, with regard to providing a service around central London and turning what was now a horseshoe into a full circle.

Nevertheless, the District confidently decided to go it alone, extending its line further into the City beyond Blackfriars under the new Queen Victoria Street, which was created at the same time. A new terminus, cheekily named Mansion House, was built (the Lord Mayor's official residence being some way further up the street, opposite the Bank of England). An extravagant banquet was held in July 1871 to mark the station opening and effectively the start of the District's new life as a fully independent railway company. Gladstone, now in his first term of office as prime minister, was guest of honour and declared rather pompously that 'the underground railway illustrated the present wants and destinies of London, the vast need that is felt for an increase in the means of locomotion and the novel and unheard-of resources that it is developing for the purposes of meeting the necessity'.

## Going West

Neither the Metropolitan nor the District showed much enthusiasm for completing the Inner Circle in the 1870s, as both companies were in a poor financial position. The District began to look west instead, with a series of extensions off the Inner Circle and mostly above ground. It reached Hammersmith in 1874, one of the many former villages just outside London that were being transformed into commuter suburbs by railway links. The District could offer a faster link to the City (and still does) than the Metropolitan's Hammersmith & City line opened ten years earlier.

Another District branch through West Brompton and Fulham was opened to Putney Bridge (1880), crossing the river to East Putney where it joined the London and South Western Railway's (LSWR) line to Wimbledon (1889). Negotiation with the LSWR had already given the District running rights over a

## Fake Façade

The first stretch of the District between Westminster and South Kensington took three years to complete. By the time it opened in December 1868, it had cost £3 million, a ruinous amount for the cash-strapped railway. Progress was not much better for the Metropolitan, which had similar difficulties extending its line from Paddington through the wealthy residential districts of Bayswater and Kensington to meet the District at Gloucester Road. Part of it could be tunnelled under Campden Hill but some property demolition was unavoidable in Bayswater. One consequence of this is the fake façade of Leinster Gardens, which can still be seen today. Here, two large houses in the centre of a terrace had to be taken down so that the railway could run through in a cutting below. Replica frontages were put up to hide the gap in the elegant street façade. These were convincing replacements and were soon being used as a practical joke on trainee postmen, who quickly discovered that the letterboxes to numbers 23 and 24 would never open.

LEFT AND BELOW: Wood Lane, the first completely new London Underground station of the twenty-first century, opened in 2008. It sits above and below the brick arches that have carried the Hammersmith & City line since 1864. The station design is by Ian Ritchie architects.

Earl's Court, the hub station where all branches of the District line meet under the impressive iron-and-glass roof built in 1876. All District services are now operated by air-conditioned, walk-through S stock trains.

ABOVE: Entrance to the Metropolitan and District joint station at South Kensington. The arcade from the street was rebuilt by the District's architect Harry W. Ford in 1907, after electrification.

LEFT: Construction of the District Railway on the new Victoria Embankment outside Somerset House, 1869.

OPPOSITE: The Metropolitan line invades London's countryside. A train for Harrow leaves Kingsbury & Neasden station in c.1890. This area was completely suburbanised by 1900.

BELOW: District Railway train at West Brompton, 1876. This was originally a shuttle service from Earl's Court until the line was extended through Fulham and over the river at Putney Bridge.

branch to Ealing Broadway (1879) and another locally promoted line to Hounslow (1883). These suburban services brought mixed returns. The Putney Bridge branch was soon carrying unexpectedly heavy traffic and helped to encourage housing development in the Fulham area, whereas the Hounslow line remained a poorly patronized country branch with few through trains, until the advent of electrification in the early 1900s. Meanwhile, Earl's Court station became the key hub of the District, as it remains today, where all services from suburban west and south-west London met and fed into the Inner Circle and central London.

**Extending the Metropolitan**
The Metropolitan pushed east through the City, opening an extension from Moorgate Street to Liverpool Street in 1875, linking up with the new Great Eastern Railway main-line terminus there before extending to a new City terminus of its own at Aldgate in 1876. Further building work on this end of the Inner Circle was then suspended, leaving a final gap between Aldgate and Mansion House to be completed. Like the District, the Metropolitan was already paying more attention to developing its suburban traffic at the western end of the line.

The Metropolitan & St John's Wood Railway, a semi-independent company in which the Metropolitan had a considerable shareholding, was established in 1864 to build a branch line north-westwards from Baker Street. It was opened as far as Swiss Cottage in 1868, out into the country at West Hampstead and Willesden Green in 1879 and on to Harrow in 1880. Curiously, a through service from the Metropolitan's Extension line, as they always called it, on to the original section from Baker Street to the City was only maintained for a few months until 1869. The junction at Baker Street was not used again for passenger services until 1907, following electrification and the rebuilding of the station. Even without a through service to the City, the Extension line acted as an important feeder from the growing north-west suburbs of West Hampstead, Kilburn and Willesden. It also allowed the Metropolitan to move its locomotive and carriage workshops from cramped accommodation at Edgware Road to a greenfield site alongside the line at Neasden, which is still the Metropolitan's main depot today.

During the 1870s, a fierce rivalry developed between the two underground railway companies, which made a merger even less likely. This was exacerbated by the personal antagonism between their respective chairmen, James Staats Forbes at the District and Sir Edward Watkin at the Metropolitan. Both men were notoriously autocratic and they had already clashed frequently over the affairs of the two rival main-line companies they also represented: the South

Eastern and the London, Chatham and Dover (LCDR). Their enmity became a major factor in delaying the completion of the Inner Circle and led to independent city interests forming the separate Metropolitan Inner Circle Completion Railway Company in 1874 to push the project forward.

This achieved little, but yet another parliamentary inquiry managed to persuade the Commission of Sewers and the Metropolitan Board of Works to contribute. With funding at last in place, the first section from Aldgate to Trinity Square was completed in 1882 and the final 3.6 km (2¼ miles) between Tower Hill and Mansion House was opened in October 1884. The final estimated cost of this last section was an astonishing £2.5 million. The entire 24-km (15 miles) circular route took about seventy minutes to complete, with Metropolitan trains running clockwise on the outer track and the District operating in the opposite direction on the inner track. There were now more than 800 trains, including many through services from other railways, using all or part of the Inner Circle every day.

Needless to say, the completion of the Inner Circle did not end the feud between Forbes and Watkin. There were interminable court battles and almost childish tactics used to steal each other's passengers, through misleading poster campaigns to denigrate the rival and almost fraudulent ticket selling at joint stations where both companies had a booking office. Occasionally, things got physical, including a clash over the use of a siding at South Kensington where the two companies met. The District chained a locomotive to the track, prompting the Metropolitan to send three locomotives in an unsuccessful bid to drag it away. All these incidents were gleefully publicized in the popular press, but neither company seemed concerned about public relations damage.

While the District remained an urban and exclusively passenger-carrying railway with a number of modest branch extensions, the Metropolitan under Watkin began to develop into a full-scale main-line concern, with goods as well as passenger services. This was partly because the Metropolitan's Extension line through the north-west suburbs was hemmed in by other railways and there was little scope for building further branches off it. In order to expand, the Metropolitan was forced to extend much further out of London. But this growth was also the result of Watkin's personal ambition to see the Metropolitan become the key element in a main-line network running from Manchester via London to Dover, then through a Channel Tunnel to Paris and the rest of Europe.

Watkin's grandiose vision was not entirely fanciful, as he was already a powerful and influential figure in a number of different railway companies and was a supporter of an early Channel Tunnel project. In addition to his chairmanships of the Metropolitan, South Eastern and East London Railways,

The underground rivals: James Staat Forbes of the District (left) and Sir Edward Watkin of the Metropolitan (right), whose mutual antagonism prevented any co-operation or merger between the two railway companies.

ABOVE: Aldersgate (now Barbican) station at night. The photograph was taken in 1880 to demonstrate the newly installed electric lighting.

BELOW: Steam services at Aldgate just before electrification of the Inner Circle, 1902.

RIGHT: A Metropolitan Railway milk van c.1885, used on goods services on the Metroplitan's Extension line. The wagon was not refrigerated and the ventilation louvres were an ineffective attempt to keep the milk churns cool.

he was chairman of the Manchester, Sheffield and Lincolnshire Railway, which was planning a new trunk route to London from the north-west. This would eventually become the Great Central Railway, bringing the last main line to London alongside the Metropolitan with the opening of its Marylebone terminus in 1899. Watkin made no secret of his ambition, telling the Metropolitan shareholders in July 1888: 'I do not intend to be satisfied, if I live a few years, without seeing the Metropolitan Railway the grand terminus for a new system of railways throughout England.'

By this time, the Metropolitan had already been extended well beyond Harrow. It reached Pinner in 1885, Rickmansworth in 1887 and Chesham in 1889. Chesham became a branch terminus when the main Extension line was extended from a junction at Chalfont Road (now Chalfont & Latimer) through Amersham to Aylesbury in 1892. A link with the existing Aylesbury and Buckingham Railway took Metropolitan trains on to Verney Junction, a remote country station in north Buckinghamshire where there were connecting services to Banbury, Bletchley and Oxford. So, by the turn of the century, the Metropolitan's domain stretched more than 80 km (50 miles) from central London. Today, London Underground's electric services only run as far as Amersham, but it is still a long way from Baker Street and a curious hangover from Watkin's Victorian ambition.

At the turn of the century, the Metropolitan and the District were still locked in rivalry as each planned a further extension into rural Middlesex by different routes to Uxbridge. However, their relationship improved somewhat after the resignation of Watkin from the chairmanship of the Metropolitan in 1894 following a stroke. The spur to progress on both railways now came not from their mutual competition but externally, from technological developments that were to reshape urban transport in London during the Edwardian period. Electrification, Tube tunnelling and US finance would bring about a complete transformation of the London Underground in the years before the First World War.

**OPPOSITE, ABOVE:** Gloucester Road station, with modern electric reproductions of the original gas lighting.

**OPPOSITE, BELOW:** Interior of the Hammersmith & City line terminus at Hammersmith, rebuilt by the GWR Engineering Department after electrification in 1907, with a new frontage by the company architect P.E. Culverhouse.

**RIGHT:** Timetable for the Metropolitan Railway extension to Northwood and Rickmansworth, 1887.

**BELOW:** The first train to Chesham, hauled by a contractor's locomotive, 1887.

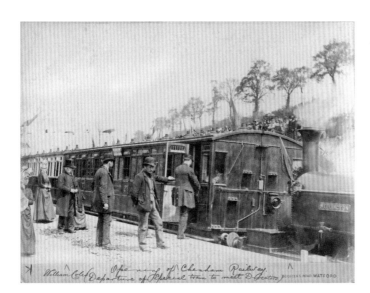

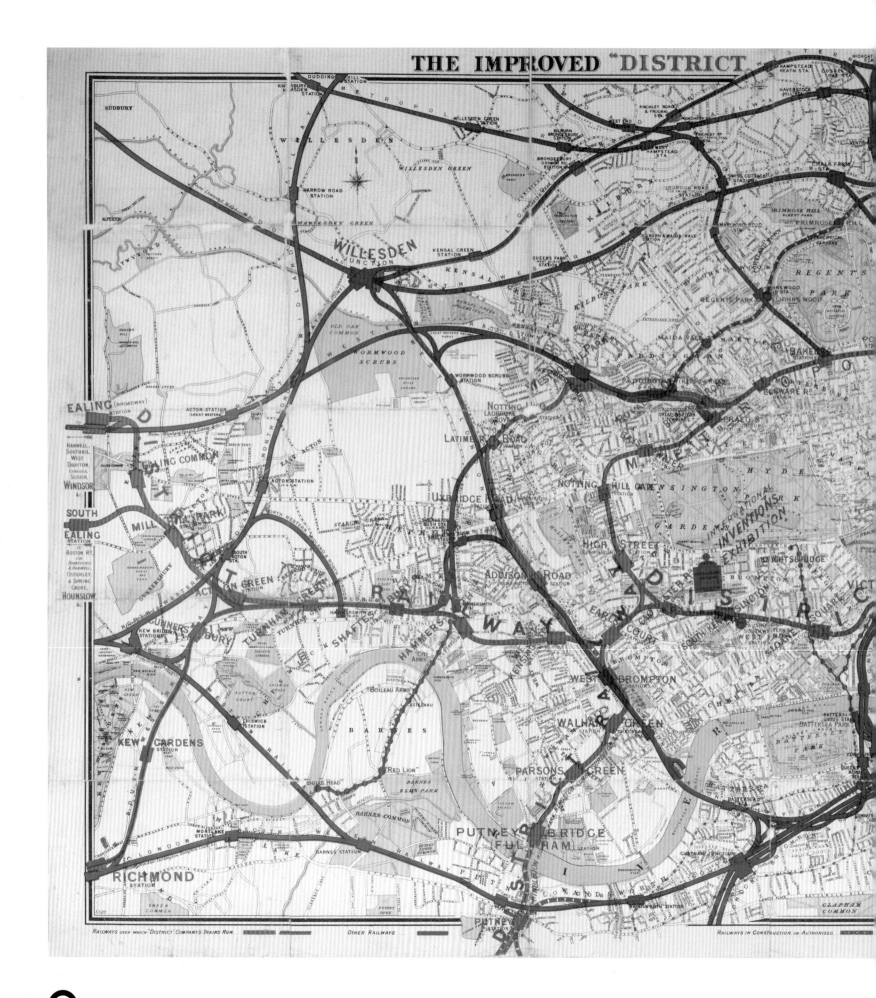

# THE IMPROVED "DISTRICT

RAILWAYS OVER WHICH "DISTRICT" COMPANY'S TRAINS RUN.　　　OTHER RAILWAYS.　　　RAILWAYS IN CONSTRUCTION OR AUTHORISED.

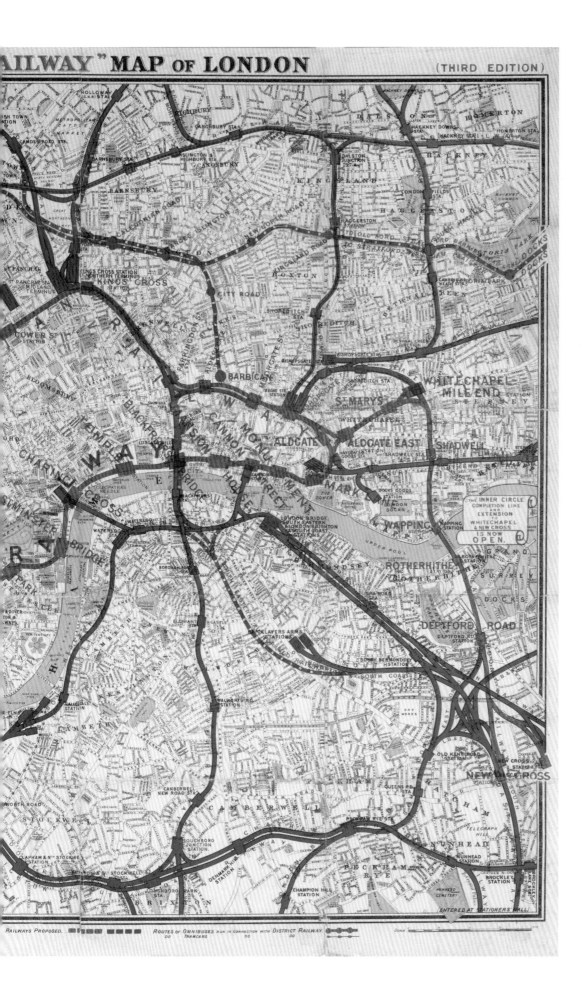

# "AILWAY" MAP of LONDON

(THIRD EDITION)

RAILWAYS PROPOSED. ▬▬▬  ROUTES of OMNIBUSES run in connection with DISTRICT RAILWAY. ◆━━◆  Scale ▬▬▬▬

ABOVE: A District Railway monthly season ticket for all stations on the Inner Circle c.1900.

LEFT: Improved District Railway Map of London, 1885. Lines with District Railway services are shown in red with all others in blue.

# 2 Deeper Underground

## Brunel's Thames Tunnel

The drawbacks to the cut-and-cover method of railway construction in central London became self-evident during the long period of delay in completing the Inner Circle. Where the technique could not be employed directly below a wide open road, it became a slow and expensive business. Neither the Metropolitan nor the District was able to show any real financial return on the costly Inner Circle project. The significant disruption on the surface during construction, as well as the proven difficulty in raising capital for such work, made it unlikely that any new underground schemes of this type would be wholly successful. Yet there was still an obvious need for some form of rapid transit in central London, particularly in the West End, which was not directly served by the Inner Circle. The eventual solution lay in a combination of new technologies, namely a method of deep-level tunnelling through the London clay and a non-polluting source of power to run trains far below the surface.

The first attempt at deep-level tunnelling under London in fact pre-dates the operation of steam railways on the surface of the city by nearly twenty years. As early as 1818, the French engineer Marc Isambard Brunel patented a method of tunnelling through soft ground using a protective shield. He was apparently inspired by the burrowing technique of the tiny but destructive naval shipworm *Terredo navalis*,

which he had studied while working at Chatham dockyard. Using its hard outer carapace as a shield, the shipworm eats and burrows its way through woodwork, leaving behind a network of tiny tunnels that can eventually collapse and destroy a ship's timbers. Brunel planned to replicate the technique of the shipworm to dig through the London blue clay and build a tunnel under the Thames that was large enough to accommodate horse-drawn vehicles. He began work in February 1825 on what would become the first successful tunnel under the Thames, between Rotherhithe and Wapping.

Brunel planned the tunnel as a road crossing, linking the growing docks on either side of the river at a time when there was no bridge over the Thames downstream from London Bridge. Brunel's shield was rectangular and consisted of twelve independent cast-iron frames, each divided into protective compartments to form a total of thirty-six workface cells. As the miners excavated the spoil from the tunnel face, the iron frames were periodically jacked forward into the earth from the bottom of a vertical shaft. Bricklayers working immediately behind the miners lined the perimeter walls with brick as the shield progressed, to prevent the earth from collapsing behind it. In this way, except for a gap of a few inches that was exposed every time the frames were jacked forward, the whole excavation was

**PREVIOUS PAGES:** Marble Arch Central line station. When it first opened in 1900 the station walls were covered in plain white tiles. The platforms were fully refurbished in the 1980s with brightly coloured vitreous enamel panels designed and created by textile artist Annabel Grey.

**OPPOSITE:** Street entrance to Bank station, now connected to three Tube lines and the DLR. This underground complex spread over a wide but confined area is now being enlarged and made more accessible. The original deep-level City & South London Tube station opened here in 1900.

**RIGHT:** Cross-section of the southern end of Brunel's Thames Tunnel at Rotherhithe, showing the pump house, shaft and part of the main tunnel under the river, opened in 1843.

supported either by the iron plates of the shield or by the brickwork erected behind it.

The principle of shield tunnelling was sound but the practice was far from safe or straightforward. In particular, the risk of getting too close to the uneven bed of the river was ever-present. Construction of the Thames tunnel was plagued by setbacks and serious accidents, which included fatalities when the river broke into the excavations at least five times. Seven workmen were killed and Brunel's son Isambard, the resident engineer at the start of the project, was himself swept away and nearly drowned. Investors lost confidence in the scheme, the money ran out and work was suspended for more than seven years, by which time the tunnel had become widely lampooned as the 'Great Bore'.

The Thames Tunnel finally opened in 1843, but as funds were not available to build the approach inclines necessary for road vehicles it became a pedestrian tunnel, admired as a novelty but of little commercial or practical value. Eventually, the tunnel was purchased by the East London Railway (ELR) in 1865 and it has carried trains since 1869, later to become part of London Underground's East London line. When the Victorian concept of an outer circle orbital railway for London was revived in the twenty-first century, the renovated and heritage-listed Thames Tunnel became a key part of the newly joined-up London Overground network.

## The Tower Subway

In the same year that the ELR opened, a second tunnel was built under the Thames near the Tower of London, using a new type of shield patented by railway engineer William Barlow in 1864. Barlow had used cast-iron cylinders when building the vertical piers of Lambeth suspension bridge and now proposed to use a similar cylinder in a horizontal direction to drive a passenger subway under the river. The Tower Subway was a modest undertaking compared to the Thames Tunnel, but Barlow's soft ground shield, engineered by Henry Greathead, became the prototype for the Tube tunnelling technique that is used with computer-guided tunnel boring machines today.

The shield used to create the Tower Subway was cylindrical rather than rectangular and much smaller than Brunel's massive tunnelling framework. It worked like a giant apple corer. At the cutting end of the shield, up against the earth, one or two miners worked inside a single small chamber excavating the clay from the tunnel face. Meanwhile at the rear, but still within the shield's protection, other workers bolted the curved iron segments together into rings. The shield was periodically forced forward into the clay by screw jacks pushing against the lining rings of the tunnel.

Each time the shield progressed, a small gap was left all around the ring between the outer edge of the lining segments and the soil where the skin of the shield had been.

**OPPOSITE:** The northern portal of the Thames Tunnel at Wapping as completed in 1843 (above) and the same view when the East London Railway opened through the tunnel in 1869 (below). Today this is Wapping station on the London Overground.

**RIGHT:** Workers boarding the single car of the Tower Subway, the world's first tube railway, in 1870. A few months later it became a pedestrian foot tunnel, which closed in 1894 when Tower Bridge opened nearby.

THE THAMES SUBWAY—THE TOOLEY STREET STATION

## Tower Subway Entrance

The world's first Tube railway was reduced to being a rather inconvenient pedestrian toll tunnel. Users had to tramp up and down steep wooden staircases and walk through the narrow subway, which was lit only by open gas jets. It was hardly an enticing prospect. When Tower Bridge opened nearby in 1894, providing a toll-free, open-air crossing of the Thames, the subway was closed to the public altogether. It has since been used simply to carry hydraulic power and water mains under the river. Despite this, the original entrance to the Tube on Tower Hill remains. This elegant little circular building is only a stone's throw from the entrance to the Tower of London, but likely goes unnoticed by the thousands of tourists who pass by every day.

This was filled by pumping in a grout of quick-setting lime, which prevented the soil from settling and potentially causing subsidence at ground level. Once installed, each concentric iron ring was self-supporting, creating a growing 'Tube' as the tunnel progressed. This is the origin of the nickname later applied to the deep tunnel sections of the Underground built in this way.

The Tower Subway was a small Tube tunnel, only 2 m (7 ft) in diameter, but excavated at a depth of 15–18 m (50–60 ft). There was a lift installed at either end and a narrow-gauge railway running through the tunnel on which a single twelve-seat carriage was wound from end to end by a wire rope. Both the carriage and the lifts were powered by stationary steam engines, which unfortunately proved to be highly unreliable. Only three months after opening on 2 August 1870, the Tower Subway Company went bankrupt and both the lifts and cable car were removed.

### The Pioneering Electric Tube

Greathead had demonstrated a brilliant new method of tunnel construction but had failed to provide an appropriate means of mechanical transit. The lack of motive power suitable for use deep underground, where ventilation was difficult, seemed insurmountable. Steam trains could not be used. There were various experiments with fume-free pneumatic propulsion, but the best prospect seemed to be a more sophisticated

cable haulage system using a gripper mechanism. This allowed individual rail vehicles to be attached to or released from a continuously moving cable below the track, which was powered by a stationary steam engine in a winding house. The principle was successfully applied by London-born Andrew Hallidie to mechanize a street tramway in hilly San Francisco in 1871, and it was soon adopted by other US cities. The first cable tramway to use Hallidie's patented system in Europe was built up Highgate Hill in north London in 1883–4.

In 1884, just as the final section of the steam-worked Inner Circle was completed, and a mere twenty-one years after the Metropolitan's inauguration, Parliament authorized the construction of a new deep-level underground railway. This was originally called the City of London & Southwark Subway and was planned to run in twin Tube tunnels at a depth of about 18 m (60 ft) from the Elephant & Castle to King William Street, near the City end of London Bridge, a distance of about 2.4 km (1½ miles). Passengers were to be carried in ten cable cars working on Hallidie's gripper system, as used in San Francisco and now at Highgate, but for the first time running deep underground.

Greathead, who had supervised the building of the Tower Subway for Barlow in 1870 and later became resident engineer on the District's Hammersmith extension, was one of the railway's leading promoters. He was now appointed civil

Statue and memorial to James Henry Greathead, chief engineer of the Tower Subway and the City & South London Railway, London's pioneer tube tunnelling projects. It was erected outside the Royal Exchange immediately above Bank Tube station in 1994.

JAMES HENRY GREATHEAD
· 1844-1896 ·

J·H·GREATHEAD
CHIEF ENGINEER
CITY AND SOUTH LONDON RAILWAY

INVENTOR OF THE TRAVELLING SHIELD
THAT MADE POSSIBLE THE CUTTING
OF THE TUNNELS OF LONDON'S
DEEP LEVEL TUBE SYSTEM

The heart of the City: a street entrance to Bank station, with the Royal Exchange (centre) and the Bank of England on the left.

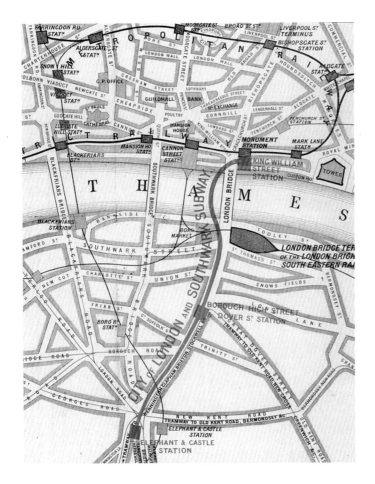

ABOVE: The gas-lit island platform at Stockwell, with a train of 'padded cell' carriages on the right and one of the tiny electric locomotives on the left.

LEFT: Map of the original proposed City of London and Southwark Subway route from King William Street to the Elephant & Castle before it was extended to Stockwell and renamed the City & South London Railway.

OPPOSITE: The cramped interior of the surviving C&SLR locomotive in the London Transport Museum – hand-brake on the left, controller on the right.

BELOW: The City & South London station at Stockwell decorated for the official opening of the railway by the Prince of Wales on 4 November 1890.

engineer for the new subway, which was constructed using a larger and much improved version of Barlow's cylindrical tunnelling shield. Greathead's name has been associated ever since with the standard type of shield used for most subsequent Tube tunnelling projects in London.

The principal advocate and developer of the project was Charles Grey Mott, a businessman with railway experience who became company chairman in 1886 just as construction began. Mott attracted some influential supporters, including the ageing Sir John Fowler and his younger partner Benjamin Baker, who were well paid as respected consulting engineers to talk up the subway project with parliamentary committees. Work was already well under way on Fowler and Baker's Forth Bridge in Scotland, which was soon to become the engineering triumph of the age, and for which both men were honoured on its completion in 1890. Construction of the subway began in October 1886 when a cofferdam (a type of watertight enclosure) was created in the Thames next to Old Swan Pier, just off the north bank of the river near London Bridge. This served as an access shaft to a point well below the riverbed where tunnelling could begin. Starting the work in the river may seem perverse, but it avoided the cost of a construction site on land in the expensive built-up area of the City and enabled soil to be removed easily by barge. Tunnels were driven out in both directions under the river using Greathead's

improved tunnelling shields, which were lowered down the shaft in sections and assembled at the bottom.

Authorization was quickly secured from Parliament to more than double the length of the Tube tunnels under south London, with an initial extension to Stockwell, making the line just over 4.6 km (3 miles), a similar length to the original Metropolitan Railway. At this point, the expanded subway project was renamed with a more appropriate and grandiose title as the City and South London Railway (C&SLR).

With construction half completed in 1888, the C&SLR still intended to use cable traction. However, a crisis arose when the Hallidie company went bankrupt before the system had been installed. In August 1888, the C&SLR directors, already anxious about the feasibility of using the system in winding tunnels below ground, took the momentous decision to use electric traction instead. The principle had first been demonstrated by the German engineer Werner von Siemens at a Berlin exhibition in 1879. Four years later, the first public electric railway in England had been opened by Magnus Volk on the seafront at Brighton. By 1887, a number of electric tramways were successfully operating in Britain, Germany and the United States. It was clear that electric traction was a powerful rival to cable haulage as an efficient and non-polluting form of motive power. There was, however, no precedent for the use of electric traction underground.

Mott and his colleagues were particularly impressed by the recently opened Bessbrook & Newry electric tramway in Ireland, which was planned by Dr Edward Hopkinson of the Salford engineering company Mather & Platt. In a dramatic leap of faith, they entrusted the electrification of the C&SLR to Mather & Platt, who had to adapt a half-built Tube railway to the new medium of electricity at very short notice. Fortunately, the gamble paid off.

The first underground electric railway in the world was formally opened by the Prince of Wales on 4 November 1890, with public services operational a few weeks later. The C&SLR was not treated with the enthusiasm and excitement that had greeted the steam Metropolitan's inauguration, but the first electric Tube line really was revolutionary. Unlike the original underground lines, which were essentially conventional steam railways laid in covered cuttings just below ground level, this was a major engineering and technological breakthrough. Deep tunnels, passenger lifts and electric power were successfully combined for the first time anywhere in the world. The railway's completion was the first step in the creation of a completely new urban travelling environment that would soon become familiar to Londoners, the modest beginnings of what was to grow into the London Tube.

Everything about the C&SLR was different from conventional railway travel and practice. There was originally a standard flat rate fare of 2d for all journeys and no tickets were issued. Passengers paid a booking clerk, who let them through a turnstile. They were then taken down to platform level in a large but slow hydraulic lift, one of a pair at each station that could each hold about fifty people. Passenger lifts were still unusual at this time and found mainly in grand hotels, where they carried guests to upper floors but never deep under ground.

The lifts on the C&SLR descended about 17 m (56 ft) from street level to the station tunnel, where there was a single narrow island platform between two tracks. This early layout survives today at two stations on the southern extension of the C&SLR opened in 1900, Clapham North and Clapham Common, now part of the Northern line. The bleak platform tunnel originally had only gas lamps, as at first the power station could barely generate enough electrical power for the trains, let alone any lighting. There was also separate hydraulic machinery at the Stockwell depot to deliver water under pressure to work the lifts.

Each train consisted of a small electric locomotive and three passenger carriages, or 'cars' as they became known. There was no class distinction, a shocking novelty that appalled the *Railway Times*, whose correspondent commented snootily: 'We have scarcely yet been educated up to that condition of social equality when lords and ladies will be content to ride side by side with Billingsgate "fish fags" and Smithfield butchers.'

LEFT: One of the Mather & Platt electric locomotives of the C&SLR at Stockwell depot.

OPPOSITE, ABOVE: Builder's plate of C&SLR locomotive No. 13 in the London Transport Museum, Covent Garden.

OPPOSITE, BELOW: C&SLR locomotive wheel set with axle-mounted electric motor. This is from one of the later Crompton locomotives now in the LTM collection at Acton Depot.

ABOVE: C&SLR car No. 10, built in 1890, now in the London Transport Museum.

LEFT: The interior of 'padded cell' car No. 10.

OPPOSITE: One of the original American-built motor-cars of the Waterloo & City Railway, 1898. These were replaced by Southern Railway Tube stock in 1940, which gave way to 1992 Tube stock after operation was transferred to London Underground in 1994.

## ⭘ Down the Drain

The second Tube line to be built in London, the Waterloo & City Railway, was the only one for which capital was raised without difficulty. This is because it had the full backing of the London & South Western Railway (LSWR), the only main-line company whose London terminus was neither within easy walking distance of the City nor linked to it by the Inner Circle of the steam underground. A short, direct Tube link under the river from Waterloo to Bank was the obvious answer. It was built in just over four years and opened by the Duke of Cambridge in 1898. Because it was a one-stop shuttle service, the line was soon generally referred to by City commuters as 'the Drain', an unofficial moniker it has retained ever since. The Drain was operated for nine years by the LSWR in return for 55 per cent of the revenue income. In 1907, the main-line railway formally took over the Tube company, becoming part of the Southern Railway in 1923 and of British Railways (BR) after nationalization in 1948. Eventually, the Waterloo & City was transferred from

BR to London Underground management in 1994 but it remains physically separate from both the main-line and Tube networks, with no rail connection to either. Rolling stock can only be delivered or taken out by crane through a shaft at the side of Waterloo station. Bank station, at the other end of the line, now houses the first travelator on the Underground, installed in 1960 to carry passengers up the long, angled ascent from the platforms to the surface.

Whether either of the groups described frequented the line is unknown, but the C&SLR certainly seemed to suit City clerks.

The original passenger cars had only small opaque glass windows, presumably because it was thought that there was nothing to see in the tunnels. Passengers sat facing each other on long cushioned benches, with high backs reaching to just below the narrow slit windows. There was dim electric lighting inside at a time when most trains had gas or oil lamps. Gatemen riding on the entrance platforms between the cars had to call out the station names and open the sliding end doors and lattice gates for passengers at each stop. The claustrophobic passenger cars were soon known as 'padded cells', for obvious reasons. Despite the poor ventilation, there was one smoking car in each train, from which ladies were excluded. A journey from Stockwell to the City took about eighteen minutes, considerably faster than the horse-drawn trams and omnibuses on the streets above and travelling at twice the average speed of the Inner Circle steam trains.

Just over 5 million commuters used the service in its first year, 1891, packing the tiny trains at peak hours, although outside the rush hour the railway was almost empty. Despite its apparent popularity with City clerks travelling in from south of the river, the C&SLR experienced many of the inevitable problems of a pioneer. As Mott admitted to a parliamentary committee a few months after opening: 'We were the

experimenters, and made the City and South London line a little too small.' The tiny electric locomotives were under-powered and often failed to cope with heavily laden trains, thus causing breakdowns and delays. There was barely enough electricity supplied from Stockwell to keep a full service running and a fourth generator set of steam engine and dynamo had to be installed in 1892.

Yet the novelty of it all was such that, in response to public demand, the company built a viewing gallery at the power station and began charging visitors eager to see the generators in action. The wonder of electricity had a magical appeal at the turn of the century and it was widely exploited in elaborate theatrical dramas and the new popular literature of science fiction. One of the first visitors to Stockwell was H.G. Wells, who was inspired by what he saw to write a rather grisly short story called 'The Lord of the Dynamos', published in a popular newspaper in 1894.

### After the Pilot

Despite its difficulties, the C&SLR was a triumph of engineering enterprise, but it could not achieve financial rewards for its investors. In its first year, the C&SLR carried only about half as many passengers as the original Metropolitan had done over a similar distance by 1864. The directors had already secured parliamentary powers to extend southwards to Clapham even

before the original section was opened. In 1893, a northern extension to the Angel was also authorized, which meant diverting the line in new larger tunnels under the Thames, cutting out altogether the original cramped City terminus with its tight curve and sharp gradient. After only ten years' operation, King William Street station closed and it remained disused and derelict, apart from a brief period when it was adapted as an air raid shelter during the Second World War.

The C&SLR paid no dividend to shareholders in its first year and even after seven years was paying only 2 per cent. Raising capital for the extensions was not easy and neither was completed before 1900. Eventually, a further northern extension beyond Angel was opened in 1907, to King's Cross and Euston, designed to tap traffic from the big main-line termini. But revenue from fares was clearly not going to be sufficient to cover the inevitably heavy costs of building an underground railway. Its social benefits may be considerable, but as an investment opportunity it never does stand up well.

## The Twopenny Tube

The next London Tube was a considerably more ambitious scheme than the Waterloo & City and cost nearly five times as much as the original City & South London line. This was the Central London Railway (CLR), planned to run from Shepherd's Bush to Bank via Oxford Circus. It is now the middle section of

# CENTRAL LONDON (TUBE) RAILWAY.

TAKING THE TICKET AT BANK STATION.

No worry about price
2ᵈ any distance

DISPOSING OF THE TICKET.

All tickets dropped into this box
No worry about losing them

SAFE & COMMODIOUS LIFTS.

**TAKE THE TWO PENNY TUBE**

No Worry about accidents

**AND AVOID ALL ANXIETY**

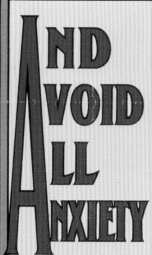

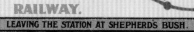

SHEPHERD'S BUSH. · HOLLAND PARK. · NOTTING HILL GATE. · QUEEN'S Rᵈ. · LANCASTER GATE. · MARBLE ARCH. · BOND Sᵗ. · OXFORD CIRCUS. · TOTTENHAM COURT Rᵈ. · BRITISH MUSEUM. · CHANCERY LANE. · POST OFFICE. · THE BANK.

CENTRAL LONDON RAILWAY.

ENTERING THE TRAIN.

Trains every few minutes.
No worry about catching them.

LEAVING THE STATION AT SHEPHERD'S BUSH.

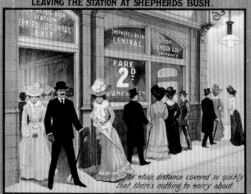

The whole distance covered so quickly
that there's nothing to worry about

## The Big Tube

Another Tube project intended to give main-line passengers direct access to the City began just as the Drain opened for business. This was the Great Northern & City Railway (GN&CR), planned as an electric Tube of main-line proportions to relieve the congestion experienced by the GNR's suburban steam trains outside King's Cross. GNR trains could join the Metropolitan Railway's City Widened Lines from here to Moorgate from the late 1860s, but it was a slow journey. By the 1890s, the frequent steam trains from north London suburbs such as Barnet, Enfield and Muswell Hill were facing serious delays in the bottleneck of the King's Cross tunnels.

The GN&CR's plan was to route the steam-hauled commuter trains off the main line at Finsbury Park and, after a switch to clean electric traction, to run them underground in new Tube tunnels from Drayton Park through to Moorgate, avoiding King's Cross altogether. The GN&CR was therefore the only new Tube line planned with large-diameter 4.9 m (16 ft) tunnels accommodating standard-size trains.

Construction was authorized in 1892 but stalled because the GNR lost interest in the project, refused to contribute to the cost and would not agree to a link at Finsbury Park

between its surface suburban lines and the new Tube. Eventually, the money was raised elsewhere, including a substantial sum from the engineering contractors S. Pearson & Sons, which had just finished building the Blackwall road tunnel under the Thames for the London County Council in 1897. Work on the GN&CR began the following year, and the main Tube section of the railway was completed by 1902.

With no connection to the Great Northern main line except in name, the GN&CR became a sort of orphan of the Tube system and has had a chequered career ever since. S. Pearson & Sons agreed a three-year contract in 1904 to operate the line it had built, but the firm was soon struggling. The original company prospectus had estimated annual passenger figures to be 23 million, but without the main-line link this proved completely unrealistic. Until 1907, the GN&CR carried an average of 16 million passengers a year, but this dropped to 12 million in 1908.

The line used its own unique current collection system, with power supplied through two outer conductor rails from a generating station at Poole Street, Islington. In 1914, the line was acquired by the Metropolitan Railway, which was

concerned at the rapid expansion of the main Underground Group at this time. The Metropolitan had vague plans to integrate the GN&CR with its other operations by linking it physically at the Moorgate end to the Inner Circle just a few metres away. In preparation, the power supply for the GN&CR was transferred to the Metropolitan's power station at Neasden. However, the rail connection with the Inner Circle never materialized, partly because the First World War intervened, and the GN&CR remained a short and entirely isolated 5.6-km (3½ mile) operation. The Poole Street power house was sold and converted in 1920 into Islington Studios, where Alfred Hitchcock started his career as a film maker.

The 'Big Tube' had been a failure as an independent operation but continued as a rather insignificant sideshow of the Metropolitan. Eventually, something close to the original plan was completed, but decades later. It went from Metropolitan ownership to London Transport control in 1933, when a new plan to link it to the expanding Northern line under the New Works Programme of 1935–40 was proposed. However, this too was curtailed by the outbreak of war in 1939 and later abandoned completely in the 1950s.

The link to the main line at Finsbury Park was completed under British Rail's suburban electrification scheme. Since 1976, GNR electric trains on outer suburban services from Hertfordshire have been running through the GN&CR Tube tunnels to Moorgate, switching from overhead power supply on the surface to the conductor rail system at Drayton Park.

The Big Tube had finally made it, but unlike the Waterloo & City it continues to be run as part of the national network, now owned by Network Rail. It is not part of the London Underground and services are currently operated by Govia Thameslink Railway under the franchise system introduced with the privatization of British Rail in 1996. The original rolling stock used on the line since 1976, which includes some of the oldest operating units on the system, was replaced by new trains introduced in 2018/19.

OPPOSITE: A heavily doctored postcard of the Great Northern & City Tube, opened in 1904.

BELOW: A Great Northern service at Highbury & Islington, 2018. New trains are replacing these 1976 units in 2019 and the stations on the Big Tube are being refurbished.

OPPOSITE, ABOVE AND BELOW: New entrances to Tottenham Court Road Tube station opened in 2018, which will also serve the new Elizabeth line. The interior tile designs are by the leading French artist Daniel Buren, who was commissioned by Art on the Underground.

LEFT, ABOVE: Tube tunnelling with a Greathead Shield on the Central London Railway at Tottenham Court Road, 1898.

LEFT, BELOW: Eduardo Paolozzi's bright mosaic decorations covering extensive areas of Tottenham Court Road were first installed in 1985. They had to be moved and recreated when the station was extensively rebuilt and enlarged for Crossrail's arrival from 2016.

London Underground's Central line. The CLR was authorized by Parliament in 1892 despite strong objections from the Metropolitan and District Railways, who correctly saw it as a threat to their traffic on the Inner Circle. Sir Edward Watkin, making the case against it for the Metropolitan, even made the desperate claim that there was no future in electric traction and that steam was still 'the only efficient form of locomotive power'. How wrong he was.

Enough investors remained convinced that another London Tube railway might be made profitable, even though the C&SLR's returns already suggested otherwise. The route of the CLR certainly showed more thoughtful planning. It would be the first railway to penetrate the West End, linking affluent residential districts of west London, such as Notting Hill and Bayswater, directly with the City. The long, straight route below Bayswater Road, Oxford Street, High Holborn and Cheapside was already London's main east–west traffic artery.

Tube construction directly below this main street meant that the CLR could take advantage of the free legal way leave that was available and not be obliged to purchase and demolish existing properties on the route. Where the road narrowed, it was necessary for one line to run above the other, rather than in parallel tunnels at the same depth. This odd configuration survives at St Paul's, Chancery Lane and Notting Hill Gate stations, where the eastbound and westbound tunnels of

the Central line still run above one another and not side by side. Another feature of the line is the provision of a rising gradient at the approach to each station platform to assist braking and a sharper falling gradient just beyond the platform to aid acceleration. Construction began in 1896, with the formidable trio of Fowler, Greathead and Baker as engineers. Of the three, only the youngest, Baker, lived to see the railway completed and opened in 1900.

Everyone seemed to particularly like the trains, perhaps because they were such a swanky contrast to the cramped old C&SLR, always referred to by *Punch* magazine as the 'sardine box railway'. Alfred Harmsworth's new popular newspaper, the *Daily Mail*, was particularly gushing in its reports on the new line, praising the 'palatial, luxuriously upholstered passenger cars' of the 'long, brilliantly lighted train'. *The Times* complimented the 'American fashion' of the open saloon cars, which followed the design style and layout of US passenger cars, although the trains were in fact built in Manchester. Everything here was up to date and electric, including the lifts and the station lighting, all supplied by a power house at Wood Lane that survives today, cleaned up and converted to form part of the new bus station between the Westfield shopping centre and the new Wood Lane Underground station.

It was the *Daily Mail* that first came up with the catchy title 'Twopenny Tube' just five days after the public opening.

Looking north up Regent Street from Oxford Circus, where the main Tube access is still by steps from the street to the booking hall built directly below the road junction in the 1960s for the Victoria line. The new Elizabeth line will have much improved access nearby from 2021.

The press nickname was quickly adopted by the railway itself for advertising and publicity, and was soon widely used in songs, games, toys and plays, becoming an instant part of popular culture. Even Gilbert and Sullivan changed the lyrics to their 1900 revival of the comic opera *Patience* from 'a man travelling on a threepenny bus' to 'the very delectable, highly respectable, Twopenny Tube young man'. It was an expression that everyone in London immediately understood.

Within weeks, 100,000 passengers were travelling on the Twopenny Tube every day. By the end of 1900, almost 15 million had been carried across the heart of London, more than eight times the first year's total on the C&SLR, and ordinary shareholders got their first financial dividend of 2.5 per cent. The 'Tube' had definitely arrived, with a capital 'T'.

The one serious miscalculation made in the planning of the CLR was the choice of heavy, unsprung electric locomotives to pull the trains. Something more powerful than the C&SLR's primitive little engines was clearly necessary to work the longer trains, but the choice of cumbersome US-built 'camel back' electric locomotives was a big mistake. Their great weight and poor suspension soon led to complaints about vibration and the risk of property damage claims. Within three years, the locomotives had to be replaced by lighter and more flexible multiple units, another US innovation that should have been adopted in the first place.

The multiple-unit system was devised in the United States by Frank Sprague, who first applied it when electrifying the South Side Elevated Railroad in Chicago in 1892. Motors and control equipment on this system were fitted to passenger cars at both ends of a train, linked by a low-voltage control circuit. This enabled operation from one controller in the cab of the leading car. With a cab at both ends of a train, it could be driven in either direction like a tram, an innovation already applied to streetcars in the United States. This made locomotives redundant, which was an important step forward for rapid transit and underground railways with tight timetables, because there was no longer the rigmarole of running a locomotive around the train at the terminus before making a return journey. The driver of a multiple-unit train simply walked to the cab at the other end to make the return journey in reverse, and the whole operation was speeded up and simplified.

In 1903, the CLR became the first railway in Britain to be worked entirely by multiple-unit trains. These were also the first to be equipped with a 'dead man's handle' controller as a safety device in each cab. This was another ingenious US invention that stopped the train by automatically applying the brakes if the driver should collapse for some reason and release his grip on the controls.

Sprague's multiple-unit control system was adopted by all later London Tube lines and for the larger electric trains

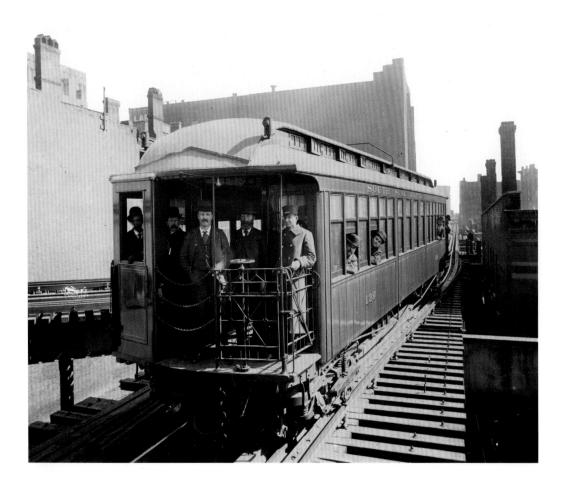

LEFT: A trial run on Yerkes' South Shore Elevated Railroad in Chicago, 1898. Frank Sprague, inventor of the multiple-unit control system later used on nearly all metro systems, is standing second from the left.

OPPOSITE, ABOVE: Heavy electric locomotive haulage used on the Central London Railway (CLR) when it opened in 1900.

OPPOSITE, BELOW: CLR staff pose at the Wood Lane depot with one of the new multiple-unit trains that took over on the Twopenny Tube in 1903.

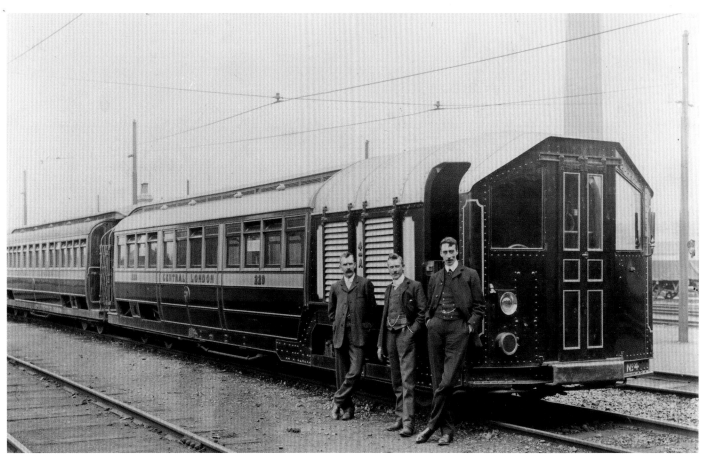

OPPOSITE: The original CLR station at Oxford Circus, designed to have apartments or offices above the booking office and lifts, 1900. A separate entrance was built for the Bakerloo Tube across the street in 1906 as the lines were then independently run.

BELOW: New technology comes to Shepherd's Bush, west London, c.1903. The Twopenny Tube (centre) opened in 1900 and electric trams (centre left) were introduced in 1901. The Victorian horse bus (foreground) would give way to an Edwardian motor-bus within a decade.

introduced by the Metropolitan and District Railways when they were electrified in 1903–05. Power supply and current collection arrangements, which varied between the early electric lines opened by different companies, were gradually standardized. Today, there are still variations in the type of trains used on different London Underground lines, but all of them are multiple units.

The combination of City commuter traffic in the rush hour and leisure travel, particularly among middle-class women who found the CLR convenient for the West End theatres and shops, gave the Twopenny Tube a wide customer base. The line provided a new boost to shops that were well established in Oxford Street and Regent Street, such as Liberty's and DH Evans. More significantly, it brought custom to the flourishing new Oxford Street department stores, including Peter Robinson and Bourne & Hollingsworth. US retailer Gordon Selfridge, who set up his giant Oxford Street emporium in 1909, recognized the promotional benefits of the CLR and lobbied the railway (unsuccessfully) to get Bond Street, the nearest station to his store, renamed Selfridges.

3 Twentieth-Century Electric

PREVIOUS PAGES: Kilburn Park
station on the Bakerloo extension
opened in 1915.

OPPOSITE: Piccadilly Gate stock car
platform end, 1906.

RIGHT: Rivals to the Tube lined up in
1913. An MET electric tram, a B-type
motor-bus and a taxicab. By 1914
the horse had almost disappeared
from passenger transport on the
streets though it was still used to
haul goods vehicles.

## Edwardian Progress

In January 1901, seven months after opening the Central London Railway, the Prince of Wales succeeded his mother, Queen Victoria, to the throne. As King Edward VII, he never travelled by Tube again, but the ten years of his reign witnessed dramatic developments on London's underground railways. Greater London's population had by this time risen to some 6.5 million. It was still the largest city in the world and transport improvements in the first decade of the twentieth century would make its population the most mobile. The process of suburban expansion, encouraged in particular by the electrified underground, electric trams and later motor buses, was well under way. Once the feverish activity of the Edwardian period was over, it would be fifty years before another underground line was built below central London.

Edwardian London quickly became a grand imperial metropolis. At this time, new transport developments were based not only on new technology but also on new money, where complex international syndicates led by bankers and financiers set the pace rather than the old Victorian railway barons, who had either died or been ousted by people who took a different approach to big railway engineering projects. Henry Greathead, Sir John Fowler, Benjamin Baker, Sir Edward Watkin and James Staats Forbes were all key figures of the previous generation who died or retired between 1891 and 1901.

The question now was not how to develop the electric underground, but how to pay for it. Most of the technical issues had been solved, many thanks to creative US electrical engineers such as Frank Sprague and Thomas Edison, who were generally more entrepreneurial than their British counterparts. But finding the funding for expensive capital projects such as new Tubes was not easy. Parliament still saw railways as private enterprises and wanted to keep a light touch on regulation without any direct state financial involvement.

A Royal Commission on London Traffic sat between 1903 and 1905 to consider the best way forward for transport in the metropolis, but its final report offered no firm conclusions about how any new systems, including electric trams and Tubes, should be managed and coordinated. The Commission was surprisingly confident that London would continue to muddle through: 'Private enterprise can, we hope, be relied on to provide as many railways as are required, provided that such railways are made and worked, as in our judgment they should be, on a commercial basis.' This was very different from the strong municipal involvement in metro development in Paris, Berlin and New York, which all opened new electric rapid-transit underground lines at the turn of the century.

Local authorities in Britain were less interested in, and could not have afforded, municipal control or funding for new Tube railways under their city centres. The London County Council

(LCC) certainly saw the provision of cheap public transport as part of its progressive drive to improve living and working conditions in the city, but chose to invest in electric trams not Tubes. The LCC built one shallow subway to take its electric trams under the new Kingsway and below Aldwych to the Embankment, but this was the only underground transport infrastructure that the council paid for.

As a result, funding arrangements in the 1900s for both the electrification of the steam underground and the construction of further new Tubes were haphazard and uncoordinated, with proposals coming mainly from overseas, and principally US, sources. The electrification of the District Railway and three more approved Tube projects that were having difficulty raising capital took place in an atmosphere of financial fraud and trickery. The principal architect of the transformation, whose methods were at least dubious if not dishonest, was the US entrepreneur and businessman Charles Tyson Yerkes, who had made a fortune acquiring and promoting urban transit systems in Chicago. Yerkes once described his business method as simply to 'buy up old junk, fix it up a little and unload it upon other fellows'. Having been virtually driven out of Chicago for bribery and corruption in his manipulation of the city's street railway contracts, Yerkes came to London to try his luck.

He began by acquiring a controlling interest in the struggling District Railway in 1901, expertly applying the power of the

wealthy US financial syndicates he represented. The District was easy prey at this point, under pressure to electrify its sulphurous system but unable to raise the funds to do so. Forbes, who had been the railway's managing director for nearly thirty years, was persuaded to retire and the old steam underground company was taken down a new, modernizing track into the twentieth century. Yerkes and his associates immediately set up the Metropolitan District Electric Traction Company to build a power station and electrify the railway. They already had plans to create additional Tube lines in London and to acquire electric tramways, all powered from one giant generating station.

Yerkes recognized there was a tremendous opportunity to create an electric rapid-transit network on a much larger scale than that in Chicago, and believed he could overcome the long-held divisions and rivalries that had held back progress and integration in London. His influence was first felt in the battle over the rival electrification proposals for the steam underground, which were already under way between the Metropolitan and the District. Yerkes turned down the untried Hungarian Ganz overhead system favoured by the Metropolitan and insisted on the direct current conductor rail system that had been tried and tested on his elevated lines in Chicago.

The Metropolitan challenged Yerkes' decision over an electrification method for its joint lines and appealed to the

Board of Trade, which referred the matter to arbitration. A tribunal sat for twelve days in 1901 and eventually agreed with Yerkes. The Metropolitan was forced to accept the verdict, as electrifying the shared Inner Circle on two different systems was clearly unworkable, but this clash suggested that the long-standing rivalry between the railways was not over.

Rejecting a takeover bid by Yerkes in his moment of triumph, the Metropolitan proceeded with its own electrification on a 600V DC system similar to the District, but insisted on building its own power station alongside the works at Neasden, which opened on 1 December 1904. Exactly one month later, the Metropolitan introduced its first electric services, using new multiple-unit trains running between Baker Street and Uxbridge via Harrow. The newly built branch from Harrow to Uxbridge had opened six months previously, with steam trains providing the initial service until the power supply was available from Neasden. The main Extension line of the Metropolitan was not initially electrified beyond Harrow. From 1 November 1906, all long-distance Metropolitan trains from Baker Street to Chesham, Aylesbury and Verney Junction were hauled by electric locomotives as far as Wembley Park, where steam locomotives took over. Harrow became the engine change point in 1908. The Metropolitan could proudly claim to be the first railway in England to operate main-line electric passenger trains with locomotives.

Meanwhile, the introduction of electric services on the Inner Circle had taken place in stages during the summer of 1905. A full electric service was in operation by September, although the inevitable teething problems of ensuring compatibility between two different power systems on a jointly worked railway continued for some time. Electric trains also took over from steam on another joint railway, the Hammersmith & City branch, in 1906. This was electrified by the Great Western Railway but operated by the Metropolitan, an arrangement that worked far more smoothly than the continuing tense partnership between the Metropolitan and the District. Finally, in 1913, the Metropolitan also electrified another acquisition, the East London Railway.

By the autumn of 1905, the District's smart new electric trains, painted maroon with gold lettering, were running right through central London as far as East Ham in one direction and over the railway's various western branches to Wimbledon, Richmond, Hounslow and Ealing in the other direction. A new overground extension from Acton to South Harrow, which had been used to test the first electric trains, was also brought into regular use. In the east, a new 3.2 km (2 mile) extension called the Whitechapel & Bow Railway linked the District with the main line of the London, Tilbury & Southend Railway (LT&SR). This was another joint venture, operated by District steam trains when it opened in 1902 but electrified in 1905 as far

**OPPOSITE:** The Hammersmith & City line terminus, rebuilt to a design by the GWR architect in 1907 after the line was electrified by the Metropolitan.

**BELOW:** Charles Tyson Yerkes at his desk c.1903.

**RIGHT, ABOVE:** An electric-locomotive-hauled service on the Metropolitan Extension Line at Harrow c.1907, when this was the changeover point to steam.

**RIGHT, BELOW:** Verney Junction in Buckinghamshire, the outer limit of the Metropolitan line, c.1930. By this time electrification had reached Rickmansworth and, after a three-minute locomotive change, trains from Baker Street were brought on into the Chilterns by steam.

## The Chelsea Monster

A giant generating station at Lots Road, Chelsea, became quite literally the power house for all Yerkes' transit schemes. It was the largest electrical generating station in Europe when it was built in 1902–05. The design of Lots Road and the electrification of the District and three new Tubes were carried out under the direction of James Russell Chapman, an experienced US electrical engineer who became one of the chief officers in Yerkes' new holding company, the Underground Electric Railways of London (UERL). Yerkes himself had little knowledge of the new technology, but he was good at hiring the best people to carry out the work for him.

Chapman was one of the leading experts in the field, having successfully electrified more than 640 km (400 miles) of overhead and street railway in Chicago for Yerkes since 1895. He was put in charge of all Yerkes' electrical engineering work in London, working with a small, tightly knit team of US assistants, who not surprisingly followed the latest US practice very closely. The four-rail DC electric system recommended by Chapman for the District and the three Yerkes Tubes would eventually become the standard system for the whole of the Underground, all supplied from Lots Road except for the outer sections of the Metropolitan, which were powered from the Metropolitan's own smaller station at Neasden.

Lots Road generated the power for most of London's Underground for a century. The riverside site had been chosen because coal barges could be unloaded in a specially constructed tidal basin at Chelsea Creek, and the adjacent West London railway also allowed easy coal supply by rail. The power station burned 500 tons of coal a day in order to run the eight turbo-generators, which supplied current at 11,000V AC, reduced at sub-stations to the Underground's operating current of 550–600V DC.

In the 1960s, Lots Road was converted to gas turbine operation, and Neasden was closed down and demolished. Lots Road remained in use until the beginning of the twenty-first century, when London Underground's power supply was transferred to the national grid. It was then redundant, but like London's Bankside and Battersea power stations it had become a listed building looking for a new use. While Bankside was transformed into Tate Modern as a millennium project, and Battersea is belatedly being converted to house offices, Lots Road will become apartments, hopefully

preserving the original control room, which still has the air of a science fiction film set for the likes of Fritz Lang's *Metropolis* (1927). Even in adapted form and with just two of its four original chimney stacks still standing, the 'Chelsea Monster' that shocked the Edwardians will remain a monument to early electric power in London and the vision of the US traction king who built it.

**UNDERGROUND**

**"THE MOVING SPIRIT OF LONDON."**

THIS POWER-HOUSE BURNS 500 TONS OF COAL A DAY; IT CONTAINS—

    8 TURBO-GENERATORS, running at
1000 REVOLUTIONS per MINUTE, developing
65,000 HORSE-POWER; to work
   80 MILES OF RAILWAY
 145 LIFTS and
 900 CARS

**For the USE and BENEFIT of the PEOPLE of LONDON**

1000-J 127-15.6.10.         T. WAY, Lith., Gough Sq., E.C.

On top of a Chimney Shaft.
*The Largest Stacks of the World.*
(275 feet high with an internal diameter of 19 feet.) Built by the Alphons Custodis Chimney Construction Co., Westminster, at the New Chelsea Power House for the Underground Electric Railways Co., of London Ltd.

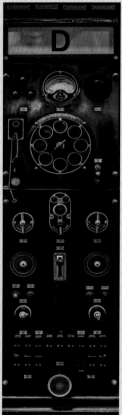

TOP: Novelty postcard of a Lots Road chimney on completion, 1905.

ABOVE: The power station interior just before closure, 2005.

OPPOSITE: 'The Moving Spirit of London'. Poster of Lots Road power station in moody Whistlerian style by Thomas R. Way, 1911.

FAR LEFT: Lots Road from across the river in 2018. The preserved remains of the Chelsea monster, reduced to two chimneys and being converted for residential use, are now dominated by a much taller new apartment tower next door.

LEFT: A control panel preserved by the London Transport Museum.

OPPOSITE, ABOVE: District Railway poster promoting its new electric trains, 1908. With their open saloons and raised clerestory roofs, these followed American design practice.

OPPOSITE, BELOW: This 1908 poster by John Hassall was the first to be commissioned by Frank Pick from an established artist.

RIGHT: Poster advertising through excursion trains from Ealing to Southend, run jointly by the District and London, Tilbury & Southend Railways, 1915. This was the only Underground service to the seaside!

as East Ham, and on to Upminster, which has been the District's eastern terminus, then outside London in metropolitan Essex, since 1908.

Suddenly, the District's long-held reputation for being slow, dirty and unreliable in the final years of steam was swept away. Londoners discovered rapid underground transit in comfortable and capacious open saloon cars that could swallow large crowds, although they also had to learn a new etiquette of sliding doors and 'strap-hanging', as the Americans called it, in rush hour. The electrified District soon spread its wings as a leisure line, even offering the first and only direct service to the coast in partnership with the LT&SR. Using small, boxy District electric locomotives, coupled together in pairs hauling sets of LT&SR 'corridor express' coaches, these seaside specials ran from Ealing Broadway across London on the District to Barking, where LT&SR steam locomotives took over on the main line to Southend. Day trippers from west London did not even need to leave their comfy seats all the way to the seaside. This unique service survived until September 1939.

## The Yerkes Tubes

Of the various London Tube railways optimistically promoted in the 1890s after the opening of the City & South London, only three more reached fruition in the following decade. These three, now the Bakerloo, Piccadilly and Northern lines,

were all floundering projects taken over by Yerkes. After their completion in 1906–07, no further Tube railways were built under central London for sixty years.

The final Tube boom was over a mere six years after it began. Within days of securing control of the District Railway in 1901, Yerkes' financial syndicate began negotiations to take over the stalled Baker Street & Waterloo project. This had been authorized in 1893, with extensions at either end to Paddington in the north and under the river to Elephant & Castle in the south approved before any significant construction had taken place. As usual, fundraising proved difficult and tunnelling did not begin until 1899. Then the Tube's main backers, the London & Globe Company, failed in a spectacular financial scandal and construction ground to a complete halt.

Yerkes seized this opportunity to develop his London business through the tactical use of financial syndicates, the methodology he had successfully applied in Chicago. He had already, in 1900, secured the powers to construct the Charing Cross, Euston & Hampstead Railway, also authorized in 1893 but unable to raise capital funding. The third Tube line taken over and built by Yerkes was the Piccadilly, created through the amalgamation of two separate railway projects in 1902.

That same year, Yerkes reconstituted his Metropolitan District Electric Traction Company as the Underground Electric Railways of London (UERL), a holding company for his

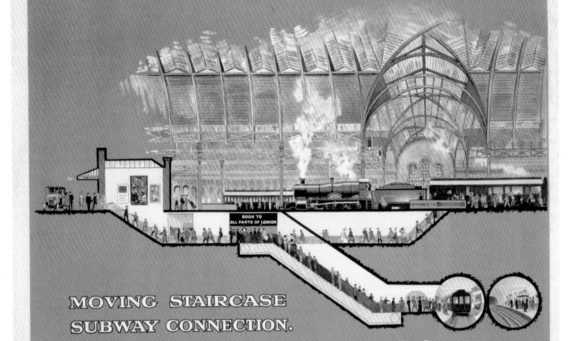

# UNDERGROUND

# PADDINGTON
## NEW STATION

**MOVING STAIRCASE
SUBWAY CONNECTION.**

# OPENS
# DECEMBER 1ST.

# LINKS THE G.W.R.
# WITH ALL PARTS OF
# LONDON.

1012·1000·10·11·13 · WATERLOW & SONS LTD·LITH LONDON WALL·LONDON · ELECTRIC RAILWAY HOUSE, BROADWAY, WESTMINSTER S.W.

OPPOSITE: Underground poster announcing the Bakerloo extension to Paddington, opened in 1913. This was one of the first new Tube stations with escalators ('moving staircases') instead of lifts.

LEFT: The standard green-tiled booking hall designed by Leslie Green for over forty stations on the three UERL Tubes opened in 1906/7. This is Russell Square on the Piccadilly line.

ABOVE: South Kensington UERL station, opened 1906. Green's distinctive oxblood tiling and faience work was originally carried out by the Leeds Fireclay Company works in Burmantofts and has recently been carefully restored and refurbished.

theoretically independent transport interests, with himself as chairman. The UERL proceeded to successfully scupper all rival attempts to build new Tube railways in London. Yerkes even managed to fend off John Pierpont Morgan, the wealthiest and most powerful of the US 'robber barons' of the day, who was promoting an alternative proposal for what became the Piccadilly line. Morgan was no slouch at dodgy financial dealing, but Yerkes won this particular battle by employing what Morgan complained was 'the greatest rascality and conspiracy I ever heard of'. The background to Yerkes' Tubes is a complex tale of business intrigue, certain details of which even his colleagues and partners did not fully understand. Suffice to say, although 1902 was another boom year for Tube proposals, only the UERL-backed schemes made it to completion and operation.

Yerkes lived just long enough to see his Chicago-style commuting service up and running in London. 'Londoners are the worst people to get a move on I ever knew,' he declared in one of his last interviews in 1905. 'To see them board and get off a train one thinks they had a hundred years to do it in; still, they are doing better and in the end I shall work them down to an allowance of thirty seconds.' Yerkes was still speaking confidently of the impact his plans would have on metropolitan travel: 'When my scheme is complete, the Londoner will be able to get from one end of the city to the other or all round it for twopence.'

He did not live to see his 'scheme' finished and died on 29 December 1905 at the Waldorf-Astoria Hotel in New York City. In London, the late traction magnate was widely hailed in press obituaries as a public benefactor. 'Rapid transit was the ideal he worked for,' commented the *Westminster Gazette*, 'and he became a street railway king in this respect not only in American cities but in London as well. We owe much to the man who revolutionized our old-fashioned methods of going to and fro.' Obituaries in Chicago, where Yerkes' dubious financial dealings were well known, were less generous, but it is probably true to say that without him the electric London Underground might never have developed so rapidly. It was only after his death that the fragile financial foundations of his syndicate system were exposed and it nearly collapsed.

The common management of the UERL Tubes had already led to a general standardization of the design of stations, trains, signalling and other equipment, even though the railways were formally established as independent companies. All three routes were intended to open up access to the West End rather than the City, following the success of the Twopenny Tube, and close attention was paid to the appearance of the stations both above and below ground. Instead of the rather low-key surface buildings of the Central, with their nondescript terracotta entrances and bleak interiors, the UERL stations were given a distinctive common identity by company architect

Baron's Court, designed by the District architect Harry Ford in 1905 as a joint station with the new Piccadilly Tube, which opened here in 1906.

Leslie W. Green. The surface buildings housing the booking hall and lifts were of load-bearing steel-frame construction, to take the weight of the heavy lift motors and winding gear on a mezzanine floor and to allow the addition of rentable office storeys in the air space above. This was very much in the progressive spirit of Chicago, where steel-frame office buildings had pioneered early skyscraper construction and Yerkes had been a key figure in the development of the 'Loop' in the 1890s, an elevated electric railway that still snakes through the city's central business district.

Green designed more than forty UERL Tube stations in central London, all to a similar specification that ingeniously combines US engineering with a fashionable British design style of the period, featuring glazed terracotta cladding inside and out, with art nouveau detailing in the tiling and metalwork. The street façades stand out with their oxblood-coloured faïence, manufactured by the Leeds Fireclay Company at its Burmantofts works. Most of these attractive stations are still in use and have been carefully renovated inside and out since the 1990s, with much of the original tiling, which had become damaged in a century of wear and tear, replaced. Each station had a different colour and pattern of tiling on the platform walls to help regular travellers identify their stop. A myth emerged later that the system of different tile designs was intended to help passengers with reading difficulties, but there is no evidence for this. Literacy levels in Edwardian London were not particularly low, and two generations had been through the Board Schools established after the Education Act of 1870. By the 1900s, nearly all Londoners could read and write.

'Way Out' signs and the station name were fired into the tile work, although the name only appeared at either end of the platform and could easily be missed from inside a train. A continuous enamel nameplate frieze, repeating the station name all along the platform wall, was introduced much later in the 1930s. The renovation of the original tiled station names leaves room for occasional confusion where the name has been changed and both the current and original versions now appear, for example at Hampstead on the Northern line (once Heath Street) and Arsenal on the Piccadilly (originally Gillespie Road). The latter has a special claim to fame in being the only Tube station in London renamed after a football club. However, Arsenal is no longer the nearest station to the club's new Emirates stadium, which is actually closer to Holloway Road. Renaming Underground stations after people or events rather than streets or local landmarks, common practice on the Paris Métro, has thankfully never caught on in London.

The coloured light automatic signalling and safety systems, along with all other electrical equipment on the UERL Tubes, followed the US practice adopted on the District. The rolling stock was also based on a scaled-down version of US designs,

## Up and Down

Large efficient lifts were the key practical feature of the deep UERL Tube stations built in 1906–07. The depth of the platforms below the surface varied from around 12 m (40 ft) to nearly 60 m (200 ft). At 58.5 m (192 ft), Hampstead was then, and remains, the deepest station on the system. Some 140 electric lifts, each capable of carrying seventy passengers, were required for the three new lines. There was a minimum of two per station, installed in pairs, each lift car being trapezoidal in shape so that two could fit together in a circular shaft. This was the largest single contract for lifts in Britain at that time, and all of them were supplied by the Otis Elevator Company, another example of the UERL's close US connections. Some of these lifts were in service for eighty years before being replaced, and at Aldwych station, closed in 1994, both the original lift cars are still in place, although not operational.

At another Piccadilly line station, Holloway Road, a spare lift shaft was used in 1906 to try out an alternative to the lift that proved a little ahead of its time. US inventor Jesse Reno was given the opportunity to demonstrate his patent spiral escalator in the shaft, which was intended to work in a double helix moving up and down around a central steel and concrete frame.

Reno sold out to Otis, and five years later the first straight, angled escalator on the Underground was installed between the District and Piccadilly lines at Earl's Court station. It was quickly established that 'moving staircases', as they were originally called, are a far more efficient means of transporting large numbers of people vertically, as they work in a continuous flow. Escalators were fitted in preference to lifts at all new deep-level stations after 1911, although new lifts are now also installed to provide access for wheelchairs, buggies and passengers with luggage. The Tube is still a long way from being step-free today and London Underground is continually working on improving access arrangements.

BELOW: The only known photograph of Jesse Reno's experimental spiral escalator installed at Holloway Road station but never put into public service.

OPPOSITE (clockwise from top left): An attendant operating an Otis lift with a 'banjo' controller c.1910; Otis Elevator Magnet Controller panel, 1906; a wartime lift operator on a UERL lift c.1917; the remains of Reno's escalator in the London Transport Museum.

ABOVE: Another American influence on the Tube: all the original electric clocks on UERL stations were supplied by the Self Winding Clock Company of New York, and most of them are still in full working order. This example is at Kennington.

RIGHT, ABOVE: Platform tiling design at Regent's Park, Bakerloo line, 1906. This station was fully refurbished in the 1990s.

RIGHT, BELOW: The original 1906 station name and platform tile pattern restored at Arsenal station in 2007.

OPPOSITE: The hand-operated lattice metal gates were opened and closed at each station by a gateman who rode on the open platform between the cars. Each six-car train needed a driver, guard and four gatemen. Operation was slow and labour-intensive, and Gate stock was replaced in the 1920s by cars with air-operated doors.

with Sprague-Thomson-Houston multiple-unit control equipment enabling the use of trains that could be driven in either direction without a separate locomotive. The trains were all to the same general design, with fireproof all-steel bodies, but they were built by different manufacturers in the USA, France and Hungary because no single supplier could fulfil the large order on time. The US-built Tube stock was shipped to Britain in knocked-down form and assembled at Trafford Park, Manchester, before being delivered to London by rail.

The UERL trains were similar to the Twopenny Tube's cars, although rather more austere inside. Entry and exit was via end platforms protected by lattice metal gates. These were operated by a gateman, who stood on the gangway between each car. It was a cumbersome system that required a lot of staff on every train and soon led to delays in busy rush hour periods. Passengers sat on hard rattan-covered seats in open saloons with no class divisions, so everyone had the same rather uncomfortable experience. Unlike the Twopenny Tube's original flat fare, which it was soon forced to abandon, all three of the UERL Tubes (and the District, which the company also controlled) chose to run a graduated fare structure. The construction and electrical engineering of the lines were carried out with speed and precision, but the whole edifice was threatened by the shaky and unsustainable financial structure that Yerkes left behind.

Passenger numbers grew steadily on the electrified District and the UERL Tubes, but remained well below the initial optimistic estimates. The Bakerloo, first of the Yerkes Tubes to open in 1906, was expected to carry 35 million passengers annually but achieved just 20.6 million in its first full year. The Piccadilly, opened at the end of the year, was confident of attracting 60 million but achieved 25.8 million. The Hampstead Tube, last to open in June 1907, planned for 50 million and got 25.2 million. The grand total for the three lines in their first full year was 71.6 million passengers, less than half the total predicted by transport advisors commissioned by Yerkes. It was clear that the UERL was not making enough money to pay its considerable debts and that bankruptcy loomed.

Banker and financier Sir Edgar Speyer, who had collaborated with Yerkes in the complex deals to raise capital for the UERL, took over as chairman after Yerkes' death and immediately recruited Sir George Gibb, the respected general manager of the North Eastern Railway (NER), as deputy chairman and managing director. Speyer was clearly looking for help in sorting out the financial mess that Yerkes had left behind and wanted a reliable hand to manage the new operations. He and Gibb worked on restructuring the company's alarming debt, while the US directors of the UERL went headhunting on their side of the Atlantic and appointed a new general manager for the London project in 1907. This was Albert Stanley, who arrived

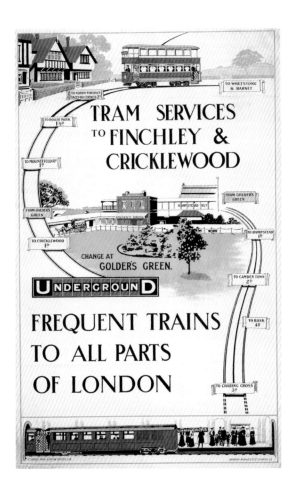

from the United States with a temporary contract and a brief to sort out the UERL's desperate financial situation. Within five years, this remarkable transport manager, English born but US trained, completely turned around the company's fortunes, taking over as managing director when Gibb retired in 1910. Rather than returning to the United States after recommending a few emergency adjustments, Stanley stayed to become the principal figure in London's transport development and, as Lord Ashfield, the founding chairman of London Transport in 1933.

Stanley's early career in the United States had been as a tramway manager in Detroit. He had no experience of urban railway operation but did have an astute understanding of what was needed to run a successful city transport undertaking. Instead of cutting back to stave off financial collapse, Stanley built new business and political alliances and negotiated takeovers. It was clear to him that the smaller underground and tram companies could not survive as independent operators, and that partnership agreements and amalgamations with rivals were the way forward. The UERL expanded, taking over two of the original Tube lines (the C&SLR and the CLR) as well as the main London bus operation, the London General Omnibus Company (LGOC). By 1913, the LGOC's fleet of new mass-produced buses was providing coordinated feeder services to the Underground and the first extension of the Bakerloo Tube had opened. This extensive multi-modal operation, to which

two tramway companies were also added, became known as the London Traffic Combine.

Stanley put his commercial manager, Frank Pick, in charge of planning and promoting these new developments. Pick had been Gibb's personal assistant at the NER, and joined him in London from York just before Stanley's arrival. Stanley already had a distinctly American appreciation of the value of strong marketing and helpful passenger information, both concepts that most of the established main-line railway companies in England had failed to grasp. As a brand new and strongly US-influenced organization, the London Traffic Combine adopted a very different approach.

Pick was soon able to combine Gibb's meticulous use of traffic statistics in forward planning, which he had applied rigorously at the NER, with Stanley's broader ambition and opportunism for the Underground. His chosen instrument to publicize the Combine's wider integrated services and secure the vital extra passengers was the pictorial poster, linked to what would now be called better customer information. The task he was set by Stanley began as a crisis response to save the UERL from collapse and grew with the organization into something far bigger. It involved applying art and design values to business planning, initially for purely practical reasons to stave off bankruptcy, but soon as a core value of the organization and a reflection of its corporate identity.

## Introducing Johnston

The most important and lasting innovation that Pick oversaw in his first decade at the Underground was the introduction of a clear display typeface. This was to become the cornerstone of the company's communication strategy with its customers and passengers. Through the Westminster Press, which printed many of his publicity posters, Pick was introduced to Edward Johnston, an accomplished calligrapher and lettering expert who taught at the Royal College of Art and the Central School of Arts and Crafts.

Pick wanted the Underground to have a distinctive print design with, as he later put it, 'the bold simplicity of the authentic lettering of the finest periods' and yet 'belonging unmistakeably to the twentieth century'. Johnston had a conservative craftsman's hatred of modern industry and mechanical reproduction, but was eventually persuaded in 1913 to take on the commission. Pick himself was a great admirer of William Morris and the Arts and Crafts movement, yet was equally keen on getting traditional craft skills and aesthetic quality applied to mass production.

Johnston met Pick's requirements by turning to the proportions of classical Roman capitals for his inspiration. Once these had been established, the Underground face, he claimed, 'designed itself'. The drawings he presented to Pick in 1916 showed a sans serif alphabet based on squares and circles, Johnston's O being a perfect circle and his capital M a square with the diagonal strokes meeting precisely in the middle.

The Johnston letterface was a copyright design for the exclusive use of the Underground Group, one of the earliest expressions of corporate identity in Britain. Johnston alone had authority to adapt both the lettering and the company's bar-and-circle symbol, then known as the 'bullseye', for new uses and applications. Johnston Sans is still used today in a modified form adapted for digital applications and a range of fonts. New Johnston remains crisp and distinctive, particularly in combination with the roundel logo, where it appears on station names and bus stops all over London. It is still both classic and modern, just as it was in the original hand-drawn display lettering introduced a century ago.

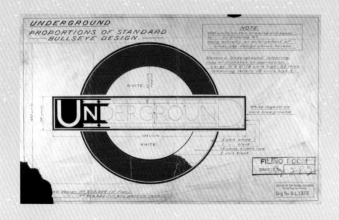

The UERL quickly got a reputation for its attractive publicity and design, especially thanks to Pick's artistic poster commissions and clear signage. In 1908, the first distinctive station platform signs were introduced: large red enamel discs with the station name in white on a blue crossbar. At the same time, the first free pocket maps of the system were issued, with colour-coded lines and initial moves towards through ticketing between them. Identical illuminated vertical 'Underground' signs with distinctive lettering were put up outside every station, which cleverly suggested a single unified service when in fact it was still run by different companies.

These were early days for Pick's vision of a well-designed and welcoming Underground that aspired to cover its costs. However, the UERL was, at least, rapidly shedding the image of a brash US invader of the metropolis, which had tainted its beginnings under Yerkes. Although few people in Britain believed in the concept of electric railway and streetcar suburbs that Yerkes brought to London at the turn of the century, early signs of this phenomenon emerged soon after the opening of the Hampstead Tube. The terminus at Golders Green was the only place where one of the new Tubes came to the surface in open country just beyond the built-up area.

The sites for the station and depot were carefully chosen on Yerkes' advice, with future residential development around them in mind. When they opened in 1907, beside a country crossroads, there was little to be seen nearby over the fields except the tower of the new London Crematorium on the horizon. But a few years later, a thriving new community had emerged there, complete with shopping parades, churches, landscaped park, cinema and the grand Hippodrome theatre and music hall. By 1914, more than 3,600 new homes had been built within easy walking distance of the station and Hampstead Garden Suburb had been established nearby. Pick and his wife even moved into a new Arts and Crafts-style home there in 1913.

Golders Green was the pioneer Underground suburb, only 8 km (5 miles) or twenty minutes' travel time by Tube from the West End. There were 1.5 million passenger journeys made through the station in its first year of operation, rising to more than 10 million by 1914. When HG Wells looked further ahead that same year, he predicted that before long season-ticket holders would have access to an area with a 160 km (100 mile) radius for daily travel by high speed train. The concept no longer seemed like science fiction, and the prospects for the London Traffic Combine looked promising.

An offer of amalgamation was made by the UERL to the Metropolitan Railway in 1913 but firmly rejected. Under the confident leadership of Robert Selbie, who became its general manager in 1908, the Metropolitan was rediscovering some of the initiative stolen by Yerkes in the lost battle over electrification. Selbie saw no reason to fall on his sword and

OPPOSITE: Edward Johnston hand-lettering with a quill pen, c.1910. An early version of his Underground alphabet, 1916, and an Underground symbol incorporating his lettering, 1925.

ABOVE: Frank Pick, appointed commercial manager of the UERL in 1910.

RIGHT: The first colour-coded free-issue Underground map, 1908. This cleverly suggested that the Underground was a fully integrated organization when at this stage it was still run by separate companies.

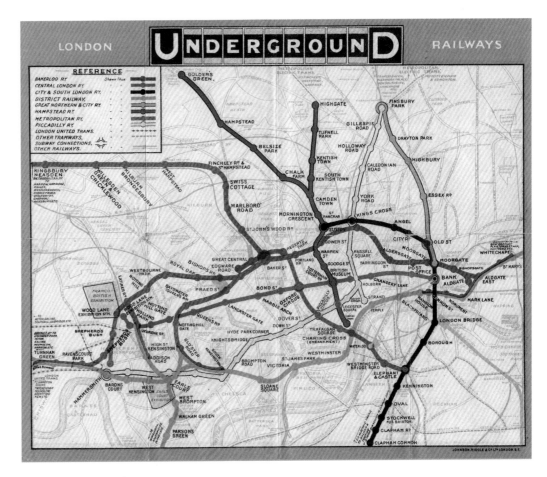

RIGHT, ABOVE: Postcard of Metropolitan Railway electric multiple unit introduced on the Uxbridge services, 1904.

RIGHT, BELOW: Mayflower, one of two Metropolitan Pullman cars introduced on long-distance trains to Buckinghamshire in 1910. These were the first electrically hauled Pullmans in Europe and showed Selbie's aspiration to create a luxury main-line service.

OPPPOSITE: Poster promoting Golders Green, the first Underground suburb, issued in 1908 just months after the Hampstead Tube opened.

join Stanley's London Traffic Combine like the smaller Tube companies. While cooperating with the UERL to a limited degree on joint marketing initiatives, he began making his own plans to boost the Metropolitan's longer-distance ambitions with a newly created publicity department and the full-scale reconstruction of a junction station at Baker Street, including a new company headquarters, all completed by 1913. Above the station, there were plans for a grand hotel on the Marylebone Road frontage.

Baker Street was to be the Metropolitan's gateway into London and the route out to newly developing suburbs and country towns. Use of the Extension line between Baker Street and Harrow became much heavier with the introduction of multiple-unit electric services on the Uxbridge branch, and two additional tracks were laid to relieve congestion. Comfortable new locomotive-hauled coaches appeared, curiously known as 'Dreadnoughts' after the Royal Navy's latest battleships, and in the Metropolitan's grandest bid for full main-line status two luxury Pullman cars, named *Mayflower* and *Galatea*, were introduced on certain long-distance services from 1910. This was the first electrically hauled Pullman service in Europe and it continued until a month after the outbreak of the Second World War in 1939.

At the start of 1914, both the Underground Group and the Metropolitan were planning for growth, not retrenchment.

After the massive capital expenditure on electrification, modernization and new Tube construction in the 1900s, their top priority as private companies was to expand their passenger market and improve revenue income. This in turn required further investment to attract more traffic, particularly from the suburbs, but the prospects looked good and the business economy was booming. Financial returns for the underground railways were steadily improving. In the New Year's honours list, the managing director of the Underground Group became Sir Albert Stanley, knighted in recognition of his services to London's passenger transport.

### The First World War

The outbreak of war in August 1914 threw all the improvement plans being pursued by Stanley, Pick and Selbie into disarray, although the real impact of a conflict on such an unprecedented scale was not predicted by anyone. Plans to expand underground services into the suburbs had to be put on hold, with the exception of an extension to the Bakerloo line, which was opened beyond Paddington to Queen's Park in 1915. Here, it came to the surface and joined the new electric suburban lines of the London & North Western Railway (LNWR) from Euston, today part of London Overground services. In 1917, Bakerloo line trains began operating over the full 32 km (20 miles) from Elephant & Castle in south London to Watford Junction in

The spacious booking hall at Baker Street, part of the station reconstruction started in 1911. The project was interrupted by the First World War, and the Chiltern Court apartment block above, then the largest in London, was not completed until 1930. Charles W. Clark, the Met's architect, was responsible for the whole scheme, which included a new head office building for the railway behind the station.

Hertfordshire, thus becoming the first Tube service to penetrate far into London's surrounding countryside.

This single new achievement was rather overshadowed by the growing difficulties of wartime operation on the rest of the system. There was a surge in London's population as workers were drawn to the capital by temporary but well-paid war industries, such as munitions and aircraft assembly. Troops in transit or on leave and reductions in bus services also contributed to much heavier use of the Underground, but this was not the traffic increase the companies had planned for. The Underground carried nearly 70 per cent more passengers in 1918 than it had in 1914, but costs went up, repairs and maintenance were reduced because of wartime economies and new trains were not available, which led to serious overcrowding and delays.

The biggest difficulty was the growing shortage of staff, as men left the UERL and the Metropolitan for military service. By 1915, the railway companies had reluctantly begun to recruit women as temporary replacements for male staff. Women were soon being taken on as booking clerks, ticket collectors, porters, lift attendants, gatewomen, bill posters, painters and cleaners, all of which had been exclusively male occupations before the war. When Maida Vale station opened on the Bakerloo extension in 1915, it was staffed entirely by women. Train driving remained a 'reserved occupation' from

which men were not released for military service, so there were no 'motorwomen', but in 1916 the Metropolitan took the unprecedented decision to recruit women as train guards. This was a skilled and important job, as the guard had full responsibility for the safety of a train and its passengers. By the end of 1917, the Metropolitan had 522 women on its books.

London experienced air raids from 1915 onwards, carried out at first by Zeppelin airships and later by bomber aircraft. Initially, the only air raid precautions taken by the underground railways were polite notices inside trains asking passengers to keep the blinds drawn at night on open sections of the District line. No public shelters had been provided, and as the raids intensified people invaded the Tube in their thousands, correctly assuming that the deep-level stations were the safest places to take cover. An official report after the first night raid by German Gotha bombers in September 1917 described what happened when the anti-aircraft guns in London suddenly opened fire: 'Many people rushed for shelter. Those nearer the Tubes went to the stations in all stages of undress and were conveyed in the lifts to the underground platforms. There were hundreds of women and children and scores of men who made for these places of refuge.' Police reports estimated that 300,000 people were taking shelter in Tube stations.

An ambivalent and slightly confusing attitude to the war was reflected in the Underground's poster advertising, which

ABOVE: Gatewoman with Gate stock at Watford Junction when the Bakerloo Tube extension opened in 1917.

LEFT: Mosaic Underground bullseye at Maida Vale on the Bakerloo extension. When the station opened in 1915 it was entirely staffed by women.

ABOVE: Metropolitan Railway female guard waving her train away at Neasden, 1917.

OPPOSITE: Kilburn Park station on the Bakerloo extension, opened in 1915. It was designed by Leslie Green's successor as UERL staff architect, Stanley Heaps.

THE MEN FROM THE SERVICE OF
**THE METROPOLITAN RAILWAY COMPANY**
WHOSE NAMES ARE INSCRIBED BELOW WERE AMONG
THOSE WHO, AT THE CALL OF KING AND COUNTRY
LEFT ALL THAT WAS DEAR TO THEM, ENDURED HARDNESS
FACED DANGER, AND FINALLY PASSED OUT OF SIGHT OF
MEN BY THE PATH OF DUTY AND SELF-SACRIFICE, GIVING
UP THEIR OWN LIVES THAT OTHERS MIGHT LIVE IN FREEDOM.

*Let those who come after see to it that their names be not forgotten.*

| | |
|---|---|
| ANDREWS, RICHARD A. | KINGSTON, CHARLES E. |
| ARMSTRONG, GEORGE | KINGSTON, GEORGE W. |
| ATKINS, ALBERT | LARKIN, ALBERT W. |
| BAILEY, FREDERICK J. | LEACH, HARRY F. |
| BALDWIN, CLIFFORD | LEAPER, ARTHUR W. |
| BALDWIN, JOHN | LESTER, EDWIN J. |
| BANCROFT, EDWARD H. | LETT, CHARLES E. |
| BARKER, JOHN | LEWIS, ARTHUR |
| BARLOW, ALFRED W. | LEWIS, ARTHUR |
| BERRY, WILLIAM J. | LILLEY, LEWIS |
| BIDDLE, FRANK H. | LUCAS, WILLIS |
| BISHOP, ARTHUR A. | MERCER, GEORGE A. |
| BISWELL, STANLEY | MERRY, WILLIAM C. |
| BLACKBURN, EUSTACE A. | MORGAN, GEORGE |
| BOYCE, ALBERT J. | NEWMAN, CLEM H. |
| BRADFORD, WILLIAM B. | NEWMAN, GEORGE |
| BURGESS, EDWARD B. | NEWTH, REUBEN B. |
| CAMM, JOHN | NORTON, STANLEY G. |
| CANNON, FERGUS W. | PALMER, GEORGE |
| CHAPMAN, FREDERICK | PAXTON, EDWARD |
| CLAYTON, HENRY T. | PAXTON, WILLIAM C. |
| COLE, FREDERICK B. | PAYNE, LEONARD C. |
| COLE, FREDERICK J. | PEARCE, JESSE |
| COLEMAN, ARTHUR G. | PEARCE, ROBERT |
| COLLINS, HARRY J. | PENNEY, GEORGE A. |
| COOMBES, THOMAS B. | PRENTICE, GEORGE |
| COSTER, RODERICK C. | RANSOM, HARRY R. |
| COX, CHARLES H. | RAVENING, MARK A. |
| COX, JOSEPH R. | RICE, WILLIAM H. |
| CRAFT, ALFRED | RICHARDS, RICHARD W. |
| CRONE, DANIEL | ROLFE, DENNIS R. |
| DARVIL, WALTER J. | ROWE, WILLIAM J. |
| DAWSON, JOHN W. | RUSHMAN, WILLIAM T. |
| DEATH, WILLIAM J. | RYDER, EDWIN |
| DOE, JOHN | SALT, PERCY G. |
| EDWARDS, ALBERT A. | SARCHFIELD, JAMES |
| ELLIS, HARRY | SARGENT, GEORGE |
| ELLSON, EDWARD | SHORT, FREDERICK J. |
| EVANS, ARTHUR W. | SIMMONDS, EDWARD C. |
| FORD, FRANCIS J. | SIMPSON, HENRY A. |
| FRANKLIN, LESLIE G. | SKINNER, ALBERT E. |
| FULLER, THOMAS | SMITH, ANDREW A. |
| GODFREY, RICHARD | SPRINGSMITH, STANLEY |
| GRAY, FREDERICK W. | STAGG, ALBERT |
| GUNN, FREDERICK J. | STANBOROUGH, RICHARD |
| HALES, WILLIAM | SWANN, SAMUEL |
| HAMILTON, ALBERT E. | SWANSBURY, CHARLES |
| HAMILTON, EDWARD W. | TAUNT, ERNEST E. |
| HARDING, WILLIAM T. | TEARALL, FREDERICK O. |
| HARVEY, ERNEST W. | TROKE, WALTER |
| HAWKER, JOSEPH | WADER, CHARLES |
| HAWKER, REUBEN E. | WAGSTAFF, FREDERICK J. |
| HICKS, VICTOR A. | WALSH, EDMUND |
| HIGGINS, JAMES A. | WARD, STANLEY |
| HODGKINSON, CYRIL M. | WARLOW, STANLEY |
| HOOPER, FREDERICK A. | WARRENER, WILLIAM |
| HOUSLOW, WALTER J. | WATTS, GEORGE |
| HOWLETT, JAMES F. | WESTALL, ARTHUR |
| HUGHES, ERNEST R. | WHEELER, FRANK |
| HUGHES, WALTER G. | WHEELER, HENRY A. |
| HURLEY, WILLIAM L. | WHITE, ERNEST J. |
| INNOCENT, JOHN C. | WHITE, PERCY W. |
| JACKSON, ROLAND | WILDER, ALBERT |
| JARVIS, THOMAS | WILKINSON, WILLIAM |
| JONES, PERCY W. | WILLIAMS, ALBERT J. |
| KING, RONALD L. | WILLY, GEORGE R. |
| | WINTER, ROBERT C. |

WOOLFE, JOHN H.

**1914 — 1918**

ERECTED
BY THE DIRECTORS, OFFICERS AND STAFF
OF THE RAILWAY.

WHY BOTHER ABOUT THE
GERMANS INVADING
THE COUNTRY?

INVADE IT YOURSELF
BY UNDERGROUND AND MOTOR-'BUS

EASTER · 1915

OPPOSITE: Metropolitan Railway war memorial on the platform at Baker Street, unveiled on Armistice Day, 1920. It was restored and rededicated exactly ninety years later on Remembrance Day in 2010.

LEFT: A jaunty wartime Underground poster by the Brothers Warbis, 1915.

BELOW: Timid and inadequate preparations for wartime bombing on the District Railway before the first Zeppelin raids, 1915.

DURING THE PRESENT CRISIS

PASSENGERS ARE RE-
QUESTED TO KEEP THE
BLINDS DRAWN at NIGHT

EAST OF BOW ROAD AND
WEST OF GLOUCESTER ROAD

began to take on a national propaganda role before slipping into a 'carry on as normal' stance that seemed to ignore the war altogether. In 1915, the Metropolitan even chose to publish a new illustrated guidebook called *Metro-land*, a brand name dreamed up by the company's publicity officer John Wardle. It was promoted as a 'comprehensive description of the country districts served by the Metropolitan Railway', and was presumably aimed at walkers, excursionists, party organizers and above all house hunters. The idea of Metro-land was to live in a beautiful home in the countryside that had easy access by rail to central London, but the timing was extraordinarily ill judged. Metro-land's time would come after the war, for Selbie was ready with ambitious plans for suburban development as soon as peace was declared.

Stanley was asked to serve as president of the Board of Trade in David Lloyd George's wartime government and stepped down as the Underground's managing director to take on this role in 1916. On Stanley's recommendation, Pick also left his post as the UERL's commercial officer in 1917 to manage the wartime crisis in domestic fuel supplies. Both of them returned to the Underground at the end of the war, somewhat chastened by their experience of civil service procedures. Stanley was rewarded in the New Year's honours list of 1920, becoming Lord Ashfield of Southwell, and in 1921 Pick was promoted to become the UERL's assistant managing director.

The UERL released just over 3,000 railway staff for war service, representing half the total workforce of the District Railway and Tubes in 1914. A little over 1,100 Metropolitan men served in the forces, which represented nearly 30 per cent of the pre-war staff total. The 137 Metropolitan employees who were killed or missing in the conflict are commemorated on a white marble memorial on the platform at Baker Street. This was unveiled on Armistice Day 1920 by the company chairman, Lord Aberconway. The chairman had lost his own son in the war, the Honourable Francis McLaren MP, who had resigned his Metropolitan directorship in 1914 to join the Royal Flying Corps.

Despite the many personal tragedies of the conflict and encouraged by a general belief that this had been 'a war to end all wars', the underground railway companies were well prepared for peace in November 1918. Following a difficult year of recovery and readjustment from wartime privations during 1919, plans to assist with the provision of 'homes fit for heroes' through the development of London's suburbs were central to the post-war recovery schemes announced in 1920. Underground railways were key not only to moving Londoners out to new homes but also to enabling them to travel back into the city for business or pleasure. This was to be the heyday of Metro-land and suburbia, where the Tube transformed the margins and rebuilt the centre.

4 In to Work, Out to Live

# BRIGHTEST LONDON
## IS BEST REACHED BY

SHOP
BETWEEN
10 & 4

When traffic is at its lightest.

## The Framework of the Town

In the decade after the First World War, the Underground made remarkable progress, developing from a still-novel means of rapid transit under central London to being one of the main instruments of suburban growth. These were the years in which the Underground grew to become, in Frank Pick's words, 'the framework of the town', shaping and underpinning the daily life of what was still the world's greatest city, now spreading well beyond its traditional borders. The population of Middlesex, covering the suburban districts of north and west London, increased by 30 per cent in the 1920s, the fastest growth of any county in England and Wales. Much of this expansion was directly linked to the provision of new Underground services.

It was the dynamic combination of Lord Ashfield's persuasive political skills and Pick's formidable management style that drove the Underground forward in the 1920s. This was in the absence of any clear direction from the government, which was well aware of public concern about emerging problems with transport, particularly in London. Public ownership, even full nationalization, was rumoured as a possible solution, but this was ruled out because it was far too radical at a time when there were fears about the possible spread of communism across Europe in the aftermath of the recent revolution and civil war in Russia and the defeat of Germany.

A Parliamentary Select Committee set up in 1919 to investigate congestion, overcrowding and fare increases in London reported that these problems had become 'a public scandal', but absolutely nothing changed. The government did create a Ministry of Transport and soon announced plans to build arterial roads and to merge Britain's 120 independent railways into four large private companies. But the minister, Sir Eric Geddes, failed to come up with a scheme to unify London's public transport under common management, admitting rather pathetically to the House of Commons in 1921: 'I deplore my inability to deal with it ... I cannot see how to do it.'

The apparently insoluble problem of coordinating London's public transport arose from the complicated mix of service modes and operating authorities. There were still two underground railway operators – the Underground Electric Railways of London (UERL) and the Metropolitan – which remained completely separate from the suburban services of the four main-line railway companies, as well as various different providers of bus and tram services on the roads. These ranged from tiny independent bus companies with a couple of vehicles to the giant London County Council (LCC) tramways system. None of them could work efficiently or profitably as standalone operations. Despite the mergers that had taken place before the First World War,

THERE IS
MORE ROOM
IN THE FRONT
OF THE TRAIN

there were numerous conflicts and tensions between the remaining operators that needed swift resolution. Yet further coordination and agreement seemed a long way off.

Ashfield's UERL group, still an association of private companies and often simply referred to as the 'Combine', was the largest operator in London but did not control everything. It ran the District Railway and most of the deep Tube lines, but not the Metropolitan, which managed the Hammersmith & City, East London and Great Northern & City lines, as well as its own main line. Operation of the Circle line, then still known as the Inner Circle, was shared with the District. There was some discussion in 1921 about merging the Metropolitan with the UERL, but it came to nothing.

On the roads, the UERL continued to run the main bus company, the London General Omnibus Company (LGOC), but it did not have a monopoly and faced competition on busy routes from dozens of independent 'pirate' operators. The UERL also controlled three tram networks that ran outside the LCC area, but had no power over the giant LCC tram system or the various local authority-run tramways in east London.

By the 1920s, it was no longer possible to plan or manage the future development of the Underground as if it were entirely separate from these other transport modes or the administration of London itself. Further coordination was necessary, but a decision on how this might be achieved

was ducked by the government. Yet despite this messy and fragmented picture, the inter-war years saw unprecedented growth and improvement in London's public transport. Bus services flourished, even though bitter battles arose between the LGOC and the independent operators. For the underground railways, this period also turned out to be a golden age of development and achievement, led not by politicians or the government, but by the Underground's own far-sighted management.

**Making the Case for Expansion**

It was clear to Ashfield and Pick that the Underground could only move on through growth and modernization, but this required funding assistance in some form. There was an obvious need and public demand for new and improved transport services. However, even the fairly straightforward projection of Tube lines into the suburbs, where the work could be carried out mainly on the surface without expensive tunnelling, was not necessarily a profitable option for a private company. The Bakerloo line extension of 1915–17 had disappointing traffic results, and a modest western extension of the Central line from Shepherd's Bush to Ealing Broadway, opened in 1920, also brought limited financial returns.

Neither of these initial extension projects was particularly expensive for the UERL, because construction costs on

OPPOSITE: A crowded Tube platform in the rush hour at Piccadilly Circus, 1922.

RIGHT: East Acton, on the newly opened Central line extension to Ealing Broadway, 1920. This very basic wooden station was built to serve a growing new council housing estate under construction nearby.

BELOW: Interior of a 1923-built G stock District car with US-style provision for 'straphangers'. This is now on display in the London Transport Museum, Covent Garden.

the overground sections were largely met in these cases by the main-line railway companies that shared the tracks. Yet building costs had more than doubled during the war and the heavy overall increase in passenger numbers did not provide sufficient income through fares to justify more capital investment. As Ashfield put it bluntly in a speech to UERL shareholders in 1924: 'The underground railways in London have never been, in their whole career, a financial success. In other words, they have failed to earn anything approaching a reasonable return upon the capital invested in them.'

This was perfectly true, but political and economic circumstances change and Ashfield was able to find the further investment he needed without making unrealistic promises of future profits. Faced with a dramatic post-war rise in unemployment, the government had introduced the Trade Facilities Act in 1921, which offered Treasury guarantees against capital loans for new works that could provide jobs. Here was an unexpected opportunity, and Ashfield was ready to take immediate advantage of it. The UERL already had a series of planned and authorized, but unfunded, investment schemes to improve the Underground, which had been drawn up before the war and put on hold. Now these projects could provide construction jobs in London as well as substantial contracts with the steel industry and other major suppliers outside the capital.

A private enterprise could not have raised the sums required on the open market in the 1920s, but this indirect method of state support allowed major new works to go ahead that were in the public interest and could also stimulate the wider economy. It was the first recognition that, when infrastructure costs are taken into account, an underground railway cannot pay its way and some form of subsidy is necessary. All subsequent capital projects on the Underground have required funding in a similar way.

Between 1922 and 1926, the Underground carried out a major modernization scheme to integrate and extend the north–south Tube lines running through central London. This involved the complete reconstruction of the old City & South London Railway (C&SLR), acquired by the UERL in 1913 but still physically separate from other lines and using antiquated trains and equipment. The small diameter C&SLR tunnels had to be enlarged and its three-rail electrification system replaced with the US four-rail system used on the UERL lines. This meant closing the whole of the C&SLR for two years while the work was carried out, an option no longer available to the engineers working on essential line upgrades today, who are only given a series of weekend shut-downs to carry out improvements.

The C&SLR tunnels were extended from the northern end of the line at Euston to Camden Town, where they linked to the UERL's Hampstead and Highgate branches using the

OPPOSITE, ABOVE: Signalman Alf Powell at the electric lever frame controlling the new four-way underground junction at Camden Town, May 1924. The illuminated diagram shows the changing position of every train.

OPPOSITE, BELOW: An electric lever frame for training Underground signalmen, c.1930.

RIGHT: Poster by R.T. Cooper celebrating the transformation of the old City line, seen as a ghostly apparition on the right, after full reconstruction to take modern air-door Tube trains, 1924. Island platforms only survive today at Clapham North and Clapham Common.

most intricate underground junction anywhere in the world at that time. Even though this complexity was invisible to passengers, the Underground made the most of its technical prowess by commissioning elaborate cutaway illustrations to be published in the press and putting up 'stomach diagram' posters all over the system. The C&SLR was also projected below ground in south London from Clapham to Morden, where it came to the surface, and a new link significantly extended the Hampstead Tube from its original Charing Cross terminus to join the C&SLR south of the river at Kennington. Meanwhile, the Hampstead Tube was extended northwards from its original 1907 terminus at Golders Green through Hendon to Edgware.

In just four years, at a speed that would almost certainly be unachievable today, London acquired a state-of-the-art spinal Tube line running right through the metropolis from north to south. It divided below the centre, with branches operating under both the City and the West End, and served new districts beyond the old built-up area where suburban development was set to take off. The combined C&SLR and Hampstead Tubes remained officially known by separate titles as the City Railway and the Hampstead line. Some years later, they were clumsily renamed the Edgware, Highgate & Morden line, before the simpler abbreviation 'Northern line' was officially adopted in 1937.

## The Housing Boom

The policy of suburban expansion adopted by the UERL was really a logical continuation of Charles Tyson Yerkes' original vision for the Underground in 1900, but with the much sounder financial base of government-backed capital. It also chimed well with the new political emphasis on better housing for a nation returning from war to peace and civilian life. Lloyd George's famous election slogan of 1918, 'Homes fit for heroes', was embodied in government legislation in 1919, which for the first time forced all local authorities to provide low-rent council housing. There were also new subsidies available to help revive the building industry, which had virtually collapsed during the war.

By the early 1920s, both social and private-enterprise housing were booming, particularly in the London suburbs. Building societies began to offer low-interest mortgages, and for the first time many middle-class Londoners were able to buy a house of their own. Before the war, nearly everyone in Britain had rented their homes, but in the suburbs there was now the opportunity for many to purchase an affordable, newly built property. In the days before mass car ownership, good public transport was an essential part of the package for anyone tempted to move out to suburbia. A station nearby, or at least a bus service to the station, was vital, and was usually the first essential feature of a new commuter suburb.

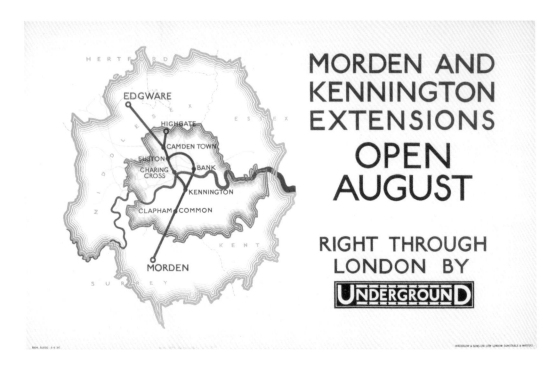

LEFT: Tube car panel poster showing the part-new, part-modernized spinal Tube line serving both the City and West End with separate north–south branches, completed in 1926. Eventually the combined network got its familiar title and was renamed the Northern line in 1937.

OPPOSITE: 'London's Newest Underground Wonder'. A poster by Charles Baker with an impression of the complex new junction linking the C&SLR with the branches of the Hampstead Tube at Camden Town, 1924. Stomach diagrams like this were the only way to show new Tube developments underground that were invisible to passengers.

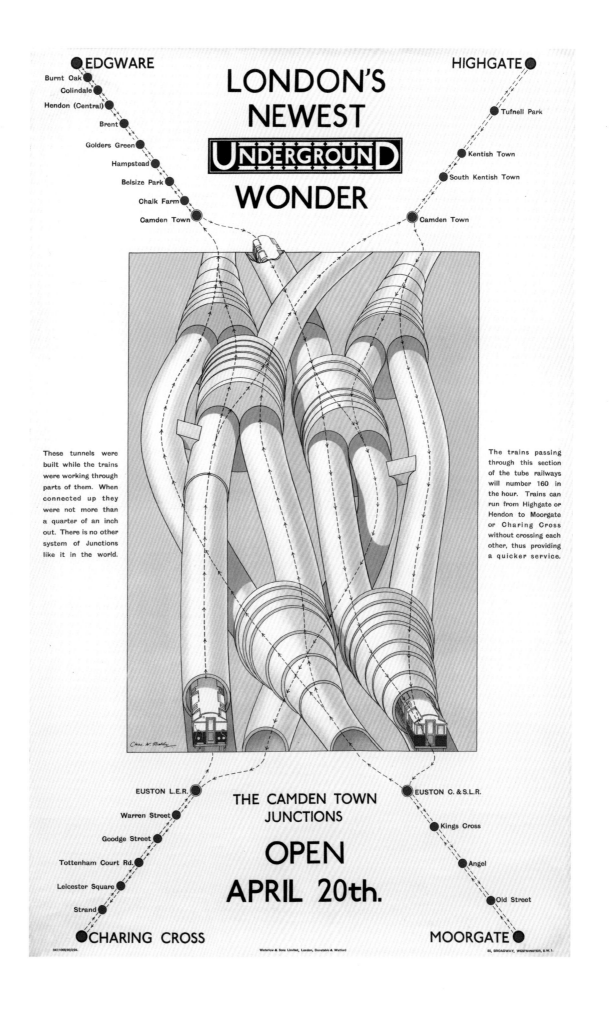

Ashfield and Sir Philip Lloyd-Greame, his successor as president of the Board of Trade, jointly performed the ceremony of 'cutting the first sod' for the Edgware extension on 12 June 1922. Golders Green, where the construction work began, had already grown in the fifteen years since the arrival of the Hampstead Tube, from a rural crossroads into a suburban township of 10,500 people. In fact, it was so densely built up that some of the nearly new semi-detached houses had to be demolished to make way for the Tube line's overground progress.

The extension was opened as far as Hendon in November 1923. Whole streets of new housing were already being laid out by private developers on the adjacent greenfields and were completed almost as fast as the railway. During 1923–4, more than 2,000 new houses and shops were built or approved in the Hendon area. The old village centre and parish church of Hendon was about a mile away from the Tube, but the new station was named Hendon Central regardless and the shopping parade that sprang up around its 'circus' design quickly created a new local community focus.

A large-format Underground poster by Fred Taylor issued in 1923 made the point about development following the Tube without the need for any explanatory caption. A gleaming new station – in the Italianate style adopted for all the Edgware extension buildings – takes centre stage, displaying a prominent Underground logo on its white colonnaded façade. It is surrounded by an army of builders and bricklayers busily constructing new homes, while the countryside nearby recedes into the distance.

In August 1924, the final section of the Tube extension opened to Edgware. The change from rural isolation into outer London suburbia was not as fast as the Underground's impact on Golders Green or Hendon, but it was equally dramatic. The village of Edgware had been a stopping point for changing horses 13 km (8 miles) outside of London on Watling Street, one of the main roads to the north, since Roman times. Electric trams arrived in 1904 and motor buses in 1913. A rambling branch railway had opened from Finsbury Park to Edgware via Highgate and Finchley as early as 1867, but all these transport links to London were slow and indirect. None of them stimulated development, and in 1921 the population of Edgware parish was still only 1,516.

The arrival of the Tube suddenly made Edgware a desirable place to live. It was an unspoilt rural area but now only thirty-five minutes from the City or West End, with trains so frequent, it was claimed, that passengers would not need to consult a timetable. Even so, speculative housing development on the greenfields was slow to take off and the Underground started an intense campaign of press and poster advertising to promote Edgware's charms. Once development did take place,

OPPOSITE: Harrow & Wealdstone station, designed by Gerald C. Horsley, was rebuilt by the London & North Western Railway (with LNWR initials below the clock tower) in 1912. This was in anticipation of its new electric suburban services and the extension of Bakerloo Tube services to Watford, both delayed because of the war. This is now the furthest point north reached by the Bakerloo but it is also served by London Overground trains from Euston.

RIGHT: A striking 1923 poster by Fred Taylor that did not need any text to explain its message. New suburban housing is following the Underground on the Edgware extension, here surrounding the new Tube station at Brent (now Brent Cross) as the countryside recedes into the distance.

Interior of a Standard Tube stock car, built in 1927 and now preserved at the London Transport Museum depot. These trains were in service until the early 1960s.

RIGHT, ABOVE: Edgware station forecourt on a Saturday afternoon with City commuters taking the bus home or being collected by their wives, 1925. This was a fast-growing suburban community on traditional lines.

RIGHT BELOW: Holiday crowds at Colindale on their way home by Tube from the annual RAF Pageant at Hendon, now the site of the RAF Museum, 1927.

OPPOSITE: Poster encouraging a move out to Edgware and a commuting lifestyle by Tube, 1924. The population of central London was already declining as Tube suburbs took off.

there was less emphasis on Edgware's quaint 'olde worlde' village character and the attraction of living in the country, neither of which still applied to the suburban township it soon became.

When the new Tube terminus first opened in 1924, it was used by 75,000 passengers a month. Five years later, the figure was 233,000. The local population had more than doubled by 1929, and new bus services to the station were carrying 6,000 passengers a day from nearby areas as newly built developer housing sprang up from Canons Park to Mill Hill. It demonstrated the success of the UERL's policy of using LGOC buses as 'feeders' to the Underground, and the spread of the suburbs continued.

Close to Burnt Oak, the next station down the line from Edgware, the LCC developed Watling, one of its biggest out-of-town housing estates. By 1930, more than 4,000 homes had been completed, and many of the new residents were taking the Tube to work in central London every day, at the cheap workmen's fares available before 8 a.m..

The next stop towards London was Colindale, less well used on a daily basis but on special occasions exceptionally busy because it was close to Hendon aerodrome. Colindale station regularly dealt with the largest crowds on the line when the annual RAF pageant attracted up to 80,000 visitors, half of whom arrived by Tube. The Underground used these events

to test its ability to deal with exceptional traffic flow. Records taken at the 1927 pageant showed 28,000 people arriving at Colindale in a two-hour period. Each train of the latest standard Tube stock used on the Edgware line, which had wide, air-operated sliding doors, carried 750 passengers and could be unloaded in just twenty seconds. This compared with a time of seventy-five seconds for the original Hampstead line trains, with their manually operated platform gates at the end of each car. Some of the old gate stock trains were still used on the Extension line north of Golders Green until enough of the new standard stock had been delivered to cover the full service.

Within a decade of its first arrival in the open fields of Golders Green, the Underground had effectively created a huge swathe of suburbia that extended London outwards for a further 8–10 km (5–6 miles) through Middlesex to the borders of Hertfordshire. Transport really was growing the town, and the Tube link made all these districts part of Greater London.

## South of the River

The next major improvement scheme for the Underground, to extend the rebuilt City & South London line beyond its Clapham terminus to the southern edge of the built-up city, was far more costly and complicated than the Edgware line. The railway north of Golders Green was entirely above ground,

apart from a short tunnel at Hendon under the Burroughs. By contrast, the entire 8 km (5 mile) extension from Clapham Common to Morden had to be shield-driven in deep Tube tunnels, as it followed the main road through Balham, Tooting and Merton, which was already heavily built up on the surface.

Tunnelling was complicated by the presence of water-bearing gravel beds below ground, which are far more difficult to work through than London clay. The stations were sited less than a mile apart at road junctions, all of which required the demolition of existing buildings before the station entrances and escalator shafts could be started. The line only came to the surface at the first open ground, immediately before the Morden terminus, which was the sole greenfield site. Farmland just beyond the station was acquired to build a new depot for the trains.

Before these practical engineering issues could be addressed, there was a major dispute between the Underground and the newly created Southern Railway (SR) about the route of the line. The SR objected to the UERL's original plan to take its Tube trains over ground beyond Morden to Wimbledon and Sutton, well into the SR's precious suburban traffic area, which it was busy extending and electrifying. A compromise was reached, whereby the SR agreed to the Tube extension as far as Morden but no further. The SR would have tried to block any subsequent Tube

extensions south of the river that threatened to compete with its overground suburban lines. This was the main reason that no further Tube lines were built in south London for more than forty years. North of the Thames, the London North Eastern Railway (LNER) took little interest in developing suburban traffic and concentrated on its main-line and goods services instead. Eventually, the new Victoria line was projected under the Thames in 1971, but only as far as Brixton. By this time, the SR and the Underground had both been nationalized and were no longer in competition as private companies.

## Pick and Holden

The most interesting aspect of the Morden extension was that it represented a radically new direction in station design, with the first significant architectural contributions of Charles Holden, who was to shape the distinctive visual appearance of the Underground in the inter-war period. Pick had got to know Holden after both men became founder members of the Design and Industries Association (DIA) in 1915 and discovered they had similar views on architecture. They shared an interest in improving the standards of commercial art and design, strongly supporting the DIA's crusading philosophy of 'fitness for purpose' in new work. Pick and Holden's close collaboration between 1925 and 1940 was key to the evolution of the Underground and London Transport's unique design style.

**LEFT:** Survey and construction work at Tooting Broadway station, c.1925. The escalator shaft is on the left-hand side.

**OPPOSITE:** Tooting Bec entrance kiosk, demonstrating Holden's innovative 'folding screen' design used for all his Morden line stations.

Pick's promotion from commercial officer to assistant managing director of the UERL gave him scope to broaden his design interests and responsibilities beyond his well-received publicity posters to a much wider canvas: corporate identity, architecture and industrial design. He had come to believe that good design was the key to improving a successful and socially responsible business. Without Pick's passionate personal commitment to a progressive design culture, it is unlikely that the Underground would have developed into the remarkable and visually distinctive organization that it became in the 1920s. Ashfield was certainly less interested in the wider concern for design that Pick championed, but he recognized its benefits to the organization and gave Pick his full support.

Pick was not satisfied with the pleasant but essentially conservative neo-Georgian architectural style of the Edgware extension stations, which had been designed by the UERL's in-house architect Stanley Heaps. He was determined to give the next project a more modern, progressive character. In 1925, Pick visited the major International Exhibition of Decorative Arts in Paris, where many examples of European modernism were on display, but he was not persuaded to follow slavishly any particular Art Deco style he saw there. In August, he sent Heaps a memo announcing: 'I think as we are to venture upon a new style in architecture for our station fronts on the Morden

extension, we are bound to secure independent advice. I therefore propose that the elevations and sketch plans of these be submitted to Mr Holden of Messrs Adams, Holden and Pearson for his consideration.'

Holden came up with a deceptively simple 'folding screen' façade, which would give each of the seven stations the same appearance but could be adapted from flat front (Morden) to a curve (Tooting Broadway and South Wimbledon) or variations on a three-leaf angle (Clapham South, Balham and Tooting Bec), depending on the available space at each site. It was a subtle but very effective exercise in corporate identity, and just what Pick wanted.

A scaled-down wood and plaster mock-up of the first station entrance (Clapham South) was built inside one of the old exhibition halls at Earl's Court. Pick was delighted with it and wrote excitedly to his DIA colleague Harry Peach: 'We are going to build our stations upon the Morden extension to the most modern pattern . . . we are going to represent the DIA gone mad, and in order that I may go mad in good company I have got Holden to see that we do it properly.'

Holden's station designs were the main focus of attention when the Morden line opened in November 1926. The souvenir booklet handed out to the press (and probably written by Pick himself) describes the stations as being 'of no particular school: it neither apes the past nor underlines modernity by

OPPOSITE Station entrance interior at Tooting Bec, 1926, complete with an Arts and Crafts-style lighting chandelier by Holden. He had no responsibility for design below the booking hall.

RIGHT: Reduced-scale mock-up in wood and plaster of Holden's prototype design for the entrance kiosks on the Morden extension, built in January 1926 at Earl's Court. The first station building, faced in Portland stone, was completed at Clapham South just eight months later.

Details of the station tiling (left) and entrance kiosk glazing (above) at Tooting Bec. All seven of the Morden line stations were similar but not identical, with the folding screen layout adapted to fit the space available.

violating taste'. This rather downbeat description was at odds with the stations' striking appearances at regular intervals along a typical inner suburban London high road dominated by Victorian and Edwardian houses and shopping parades. The white Portland stone of the station frontages was a dramatic contrast to the red brick of the older structures, and there were prominent Underground symbols over the entrance canopies and in the large glass windows. At night, the stations were even more visible, with the coloured glass roundels backlit from inside, the stonework floodlit and, for a short time after opening, a searchlight beaming into the sky from each station roof.

When new, the stations must have seemed like alien spacecraft dotted along this drab and poorly lit south London street, but they appeared to be popular with the critics and travelling public alike. *The Architects' Journal* praised Holden for 'a design that solves its problem, creates a new type of building and improves the face of London'. The design of the Morden line stations was important because they had to fulfil a more complex role than the Edgware line structures, which initially sat alone like little houses on the Middlesex prairie. In built-up south London, the new stations had to stand out like beacons to attract passengers from the existing street transport options, while also fitting in with and contributing to an improved urban environment.

## Metro-land

The Metropolitan Railway, still fiercely independent of the Underground, took a rather different approach to development after the First World War. Robert Selbie, the Metropolitan's general manager from 1908, had decided early on that concentrating on outer suburban services was a better strategy than investing in central London, where new transport provision was becoming almost saturated in the Edwardian years. He saw too many competing electric tram, Tube and motor bus services, all forced to offer cheap fares but with little margin for profit.

The autocratic but far-sighted Selbie saw more potential in first-class and long-distance traffic development than mass-market rapid transit under London. He did not ignore central London and the original urban sections of the Metropolitan, now at last all electrified, but set his sights on development up what was still called the Extension line, from Baker Street into the country areas north-west of London to which the wealthier middle classes could be attracted. Selbie set up a publicity department in 1911, which began producing postcards, brochures, country walks leaflets and even a film showing a journey along the line from Baker Street to Aylesbury. These productions were aimed at holidaymakers and day trippers, but Selbie was convinced that the railway could also build up long-distance commuter traffic if it could offer demonstrably better

## Crowding Morden

The Morden extension very rapidly made an impact beyond the Tube terminus. When Morden station opened in 1926, there was still a working farm on the other side of the road in what was best described as a hamlet rather than a village. There were a few cottages, two or three larger houses and an inn surrounded by open fields, except where the new Underground depot had been built.

An aerial photograph taken ten years later from the roof of the new cinema opposite the station shows newly built suburban housing stretching into the distance covering all the open countryside. There are ten buses in the station forecourt, indicating the wider reach of the Tube through connecting services to more distant communities such as Worcester Park, Sutton, Carshalton and Cheam, which were all becoming outer London suburbs. By this time, Morden was the most heavily used of all the suburban Tube stations, and with growing complaints about

overcrowding on peak services, the Underground was no longer promoting the benefits of a suburban idyll at the end of the line.

and faster services. In his mind, the former Extension line out to the country from Baker Street was now the main line in more ways than one, and this was the focus of both the railway's promotion and its improvement. It was also spurred on by competition from the Great Central Railway, whose smart new trains from Marylebone to the Chilterns shared the lines beyond Finchley Road under a joint agreement with the Metropolitan.

A major investment in additional express tracks over the busy bottleneck section between Finchley Road and Wembley Park during 1913–15 was a crucial step forward. Complete reconstruction of Baker Street station, the hub of the Metropolitan, had begun in 1910 and was almost complete by 1914. This included direct escalator interchange with the Bakerloo Tube station below, which had opened with a separate entrance from the Metropolitan station in 1906. Journeys were shortened and simplified for nearly 3 million annual passengers coming in on the main line, who made this inconvenient daily change here.

A new head office for the company was built alongside the new station; it was one of the first designs by Charles W. Clark, the Metropolitan's recently appointed 'architectural assistant to the engineer'. Clark was formally elevated to the position of company architect in 1921, and was fondly referred to by the chairman, Lord Aberconway, as 'our clarkitect'. He designed

about twenty-five new or rebuilt stations for the Metropolitan between 1911 and 1933, some of them prepared with detailed drawings during the war years but not built until the 1920s. His biggest project was Chiltern Court, the giant block of mansion flats over Baker Street station, which eventually replaced the abandoned hotel project in 1929–30.

Selbie's additional proposals to extend the electrification of the main line beyond Harrow to Rickmansworth, and to build a new electric branch to Watford, had to be postponed with the outbreak of war in 1914. Wartime economic conditions soon also curtailed Selbie's particularly favoured project, which was to develop housing estates on railway-owned land close to its suburban and country stations. The Metropolitan had started this practice in a low-key way near Willesden Green back in the 1880s, followed by some housing at Wembley and Pinner in the early 1900s.

Selbie was so anxious to promote more of the districts served by the railway as being ideal to live in, rather than just to visit, that he launched the first edition of *Metro-land*, a glossy and attractive new guidebook to the Metropolitan's outer catchment area, in May 1915. The timing of the publication was odd, as few people would have been planning to move house during wartime, but the strategy could well have been to encourage casual visitors to become prospective residents after the war.

Great Portland Street, the last of the original Metropolitan line stations to be rebuilt in the 1920s. Charles W. Clark's elegant surface building was completed in 1930.

Against expectation, the war dragged on for three more years. Selbie stuck to his strategy, and the 1920 edition of the guide was still using much of the soothing copy from the first:

The strain which the London business or professional man has to undergo amidst the turmoil and bustle of Town can only be counteracted by the quiet restfulness and comfort of a residence amidst pure air and surroundings, and whilst jaded vitality and taxed nerves are the natural penalties of modern conditions, Nature has, in the delightful districts abounding in Metro-land, placed a potential remedy at hand.

The initial promotion may have been premature, but Selbie kept new season ticket holders in his sights. By the end of the war, he had even devised his own plan to organize the direct development of Metro-land, which anticipated perfectly the post-war demand for new homes out of town.

In January 1919, just two months after the Armistice, Selbie announced the creation of a new property company, Metropolitan Railway Country Estates (MRCE). This was to be his mechanism for actively managing and developing the Metropolitan's 'surplus' land holdings, meaning property adjacent to the line that had been acquired before it was built but often remained unused once the railway was complete. Legally, the MRCE was a separate company independent of the railway, but in practice it was under the control of the Metropolitan's directors. Selbie, who was an MRCE director from the start, became a director of the Metropolitan Railway in 1922 while continuing to serve as its general manager. It was a cosy arrangement that gave the Metropolitan the unique opportunity among railway companies to become closely involved with quite extensive private property development. 'Railway companies', wrote Selbie smugly in 1921, 'are trusted and not open to the suspicion that often attaches to the speculative builder and estate developer.'

Between 1919 and 1933, the MRCE developed a string of housing estates near stations all down the line at Wembley Park, Northwick Park, Eastcote, Rayners Lane, Ruislip, Hillingdon, Pinner, Rickmansworth, Chorleywood and Amersham. In the early days, the estates company built some houses itself, but the usual pattern was to lay out an estate and then sell plots to individual purchasers wishing to have a house built to their own specifications. Later on, the design and construction were usually undertaken by other companies, which would offer the prospective purchaser a choice of house sizes and styles at a range of prices.

The annual *Metro-land* guide became the main advertising medium for these developments. The dream of a new house on the edge of beautiful countryside but with every modern convenience, including a fast rail service to central London, was

RIGHT: The new Metro-land housing estate at Rayners Lane developed by the Metropolitan Railway had been renamed Harrow Garden Village by 1928.

OPPOSITE: Poster advertising the 1926 edition of the *Metro-land* booklet.

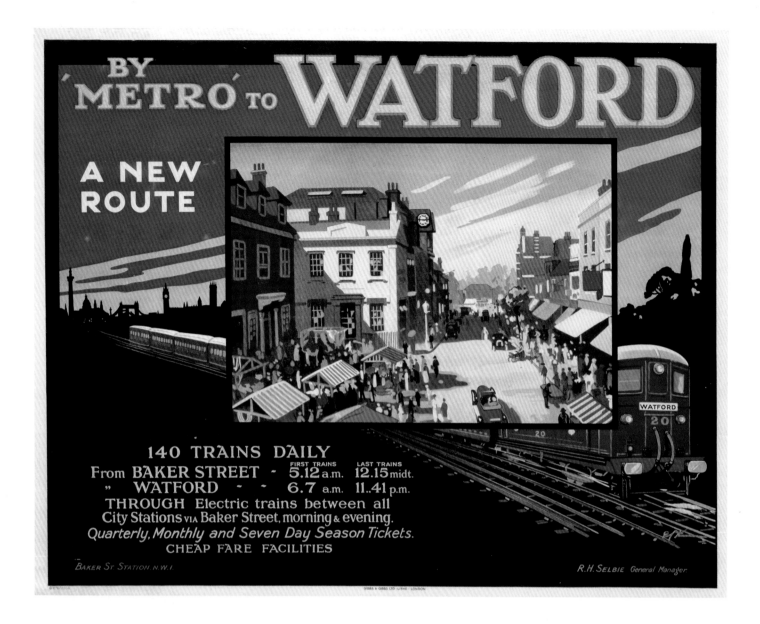

ABOVE: Poster advertising the new Met branch to Watford, 1925. The central image is actually quite misleading as the line terminates in the suburbs more than a mile from the town centre.

LEFT: The 'Live in Metro-land' message was even carried on the brass door handles of Met coaches in the 1920s.

RIGHT: A Metropolitan electric train heads through Metro-land to Rickmansworth, the outer limit of electric working from 1925. This is a children's book illustration by Leslie Carr, 1930.

an appealing vision ninety years ago, and remains so today. In true advertising tradition, the Metropolitan's copywriters went over the top with their purple prose, rather unconvincingly blending notions of rural tradition with civilized progress: 'This is a good parcel of English soil in which to build home and strike root, inhabited from of old . . . the new settlement of Metroland proceeds apace; the new colonists thrive again.'

The language must have sounded contrived even then, although a quick glance at the ads and features in the *Homes and Property* supplement of the London *Evening Standard* will show that marketing methods have changed only superficially. *Metro-land* was one of the first and most successful examples of the 'lifestyle' approach to property marketing that is now familiar to us all, and the emphasis on a fast rail link to London is still paramount for today's commuters.

A comparison of the census returns for 1921 and 1931 shows a population increase of nearly 11 per cent for Greater London as a whole, with a much higher rate of growth in the north-west suburbs located between 8 and 16 km (5–10 miles) from the centre. The Metro-land districts of Harrow, Ruislip, Northwood, Uxbridge and Wembley all experienced increases of more than 50 per cent. In 1929, the Metropolitan Railway's commercial manager estimated that between 1919 and 1928, some 12,000 houses had been built within half a mile of the stations between Willesden Green and Uxbridge, with a further 17,000 planned.

Only a small proportion of these had been built through the MRCE, but most of them contributed to the significant rise in ticket sales on the Metropolitan, particularly of season tickets. Sample monthly season-ticket issue figures from individual stations show that between 1921 and 1928, sales at Rickmansworth and Ruislip nearly doubled, for example. At Preston Road, Northwick Park and Wembley Park, the rise was more than 700 per cent. The most spectacular growth of all was at Ickenham, where only 59 monthly season tickets were sold in 1921, compared to 1,497 in 1928.

## Comfortable Modernity

Some of Selbie's shelved pre-war modernization plans were implemented in this period to help meet and further stimulate growing traffic demand. Apart from the temporary boost from the British Empire Exhibition at Wembley in 1924–5 and other special events such as the annual FA Cup Final, held at Wembley from 1923, this was nearly all commuter-based.

The extension of electric working beyond Harrow to Rickmansworth and the construction of a new branch to Watford were both completed in 1925. The Watford branch was built jointly with the LNER, taking advantage of the financial guarantees offered by the Trade Facilities Act that had also made the UERL's Tube extensions possible. Traffic was, and always has been, disappointing, largely because

## Wonderful Wembley

The British Empire Exhibition of 1924–5 put Wembley permanently on the map and acted as a timely boost for Metro-land as a whole. It was not a project originally promoted by the Metropolitan Railway, but the fortuitous choice of Wembley Park as the event site led to considerable benefits for the railway and the area. The exhibition was the largest to be held in Britain since the Great Exhibition of 1851, which drew crowds to the Crystal Palace in Hyde Park. Its purpose was to promote both the image and the economy of the British Empire or, in the words of the official guidebook, 'to display the natural resources of the Empire, and the activities, industrial and social, of their peoples'. The Metropolitan was the first to profit from the venture through the sale of 87 hectares (216 acres) of Wembley Park to the exhibition company in 1922, at last recouping some of Sir Edward Watkin's ill-fated investment of the 1890s when he had hoped to develop the site as a pleasure ground.

The Empire Stadium was a huge national sports arena, the largest of its kind in the world, built almost entirely using the newly refined technique of reinforced concrete. The new structure could accommodate 125,000 spectators and

was first used to stage the FA Cup Final in 1923. The giant twin towers of the stadium came to symbolize Wembley as the national home of English football, and they stood for eighty years until the controversial but long overdue redevelopment of the stadium in 2003. Match days are still the busiest occasions for Wembley Park station today.

The various ferro-concrete palaces and pavilions of the British Empire Exhibition and the adjacent amusement park were ready for a grand royal inauguration by King George V on St George's Day, 1924. The King's speech was relayed by the newly created BBC to nearly 7 million listeners, who for the first time heard a monarch's voice over the wireless. The exhibition organizers confidently predicted at least 25 million visitors to 'Wonderful Wembley'. In fact, only 17.4 million people had passed through the turnstiles when the exhibition closed on 1 November 1924. A second season in 1925, with various new exhibits, was inevitably less popular, attracting 9.7 million customers. The exhibition had its own special bus station and a new railway station on the LNER line from Marylebone, but a large proportion of the visitors arrived at Wembley Park on the Metropolitan's trains.

OPPOSITE: A Metro-Vick electric locomotive displayed in the Palace of Engineering at the British Empire Exhibition at Wembley, 1925. The twenty locos were all later given names and today No. 12, Sarah Siddons, is kept in working order by London Underground to run occasional heritage services.

RIGHT: Special issue of *Metro-land* doubling as a guide to the British Empire Exhibition, 1924. The cover image shows the new Empire Stadium, first used for the FA Cup Final in 1923. Wembley Stadium became the home of English football and the site was not redeveloped and modernized until 2003.

**METRO-LAND**

**BRITISH EMPIRE EXHIBITION NUMBER**

PRICE THREE-PENCE

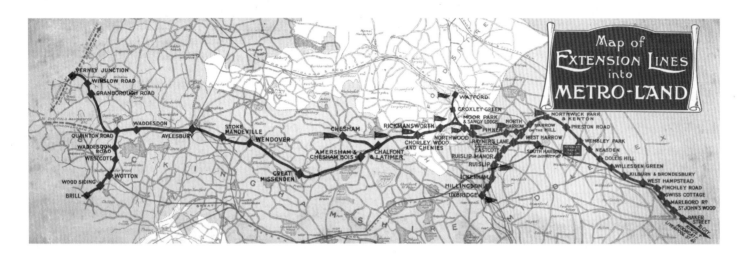

the terminus is in a residential area 1.6 km (1 mile) from the centre of Watford. Only in this particular case were Selbie's predictions of a healthy commuter market from new suburbanites flawed.

The Metropolitan ordered a fleet of twenty powerful 1200hp electric locomotives to handle the improved services. They were to provide the main motive power for the long-distance services for nearly forty years, hauling trains as far as Rickmansworth (from 1925), where steam engines took over for the remainder of the journey to Aylesbury and Verney Junction. The 'Metro-Vicks' were the only main-line electric locomotives in the country at the time, and the railway proudly put one on display in the Palace of Engineering at the British Empire Exhibition in 1925, its side panelling removed to show off the electrical equipment inside. At the exhibition in 1924, the LNER had displayed *Flying Scotsman*, its latest main-line express passenger steam locomotive. Impressive though *Scotsman* was, it was essentially old technology and the Metropolitan could therefore promote itself at Wembley as the electric railway of the future.

Yet the Metropolitan's modernity was not always apparent because of its generally conservative appearance and design. Virtually everything about the railway had an old-fashioned look, even when it made use of the latest technical developments to serve Metro-land. Selbie's Metropolitan

remained comfortably Edwardian in this respect, while Pick's Underground was increasingly setting the pace as a thoroughly advanced transport system that was sleek and stylish.

The latest multiple-unit electric trains on the Metropolitan, for example, looked exactly the same as the traditional coaches pulled by steam engines, with comfortable individual compartments and slam doors. They offered nothing like the smooth lines of the up-to-date Underground trains, with their sliding air doors controlled by the guard. Yet their antiquated appearance concealed an important technical innovation: roller bearings on the axleboxes and traction motors, which reduced the need for regular lubrication, reduced current consumption and eliminated the problem of 'hot boxes'. These improvements became a standard feature of new rolling stock in the 1930s, but the Metropolitan preferred to keep them under wraps rather than to celebrate modernity.

The Metropolitan continued to replicate, on a smaller scale, nearly all the features of a traditional main-line railway, with mixed goods trains carrying everything from milk to coal and a parcel delivery service as well as passenger operations. Lord Aberconway, the company chairman, often made a virtue of this anomaly for a mixed urban, suburban and country line, describing it with some pride as 'a trunk line in miniature'. It still gave the Metropolitan an unusual split personality that was difficult to sustain as a single, independent operation.

The imposing classicism of Charles W. Clark's Marylebone Road entrance to Baker Street station provides a stark contrast to the modern vision of Pick and Holden.

OPPOSITE: A poster promoting the Metropolitan's Goods and Parcels service, which included home collection and delivery in the 1920s. These 'main-line' services ended when London Transport took over in 1933.

LEFT: Baker Street station and Chiltern Court from Marylebone Road, 1933. The entrance canopy on the right was badly damaged by bombing in the Second World War and subsequently removed.

LEFT, BELOW: The Chiltern Court restaurant opened in 1930, but was never a great success. It is now a Weatherspoons pub called the Metropolitan Bar.

Even the new Metro-land stations designed by Clark, such as Watford and Stanmore, had the reassuring look of small country houses, with deep Arts and Crafts-style roofs and built-in residential accommodation. Chiltern Court, the enormous block of flats built over Baker Street station, was finally completed in 1929, by which time it had the slightly dated and overpowering style of a grand Edwardian hotel. It boasted its own large restaurant, which was run by the caterers Spiers & Pond. The higher-class restaurant at Chiltern Court, which was not aimed at railway passengers, was a financial disaster and was soon losing money at an alarming rate. It survives today as a Wetherspoons pub called the Metropolitan Bar, with the coats of arms of the towns and counties served by the line still adorning the pilasters of the main room.

Appropriately enough, two early tenants of the apartments at Baker Street were the well-established Edwardian writers H.G. Wells and Arnold Bennett, by then past their prime. Inevitably, *Metro-land* claimed that the apartment block was the largest and most luxurious in London, which 'opened a new chapter of advance in residential flat technique', but Chiltern Court was certainly not fashionable. A comparison with the new Underground Group headquarters at 55 Broadway (see pages 146–7), designed by Holden, which was built at the same time, demonstrates the widening stylistic contrast that was opening up between the Underground and the Metropolitan.

# 5 Combining it All

SWAN & EDGAR'S

COUNTY FIRE OFFICE

MONICO

THE LONDON PAVILION

BOVRIL

SCHWEPPES GINGER ALE

SHAFTESBURY AVENUE

BOOKING HALL

ENTRANCE

ENTRANCE

ENTRANCE

REGENT STREET

ENTRANCE

SHOW CASES

Bookstall

Tobacco, fruit & Confectionery Stalls

Bookstall

SHOW CASES

LOWER REGENT ST.

Switch House

CIRCULATING AREA

ENTRANCE

MACHINERY FLOOR

ENTRANCE

CHANGE KIOSKS & AUTOMATIC BOOKING OFFICE

5 ESCALATORS

EAST BOUND

AUXILIARY BOOKING OFFICE

PIPE

SUBWAY

3 ESCALATORS (PICCADILLY)

INTERCHANGE

3 ESCALATORS (BAKERLOO)

PICCADILLY

STAIRCASE TO STREET

WEST BOUND

NORTH BOUND

SOUTH BOUND

D. MACPHERSON

**PREVIOUS PAGES:** The elegant Art Deco lighting of 1938 Tube stock. The sprung hand grabs found a new use in the Second World War when they were issued to commando troops as coshes.

**OPPOSITE:** The Underground's showpiece development of 1928. A cutaway view of the new Piccadilly Circus station after reconstruction.

**LEFT:** The opening ceremony at Piccadilly in December 1928 with the Mayor Of Westminster about to switch on an Art Deco lamp and activate the escalators. Underground chairman Lord Ashfield is on the Mayor's right.

**ABOVE:** The World Time Today. A map of the world with moving time zones installed at Piccadilly in 1928 and still operational today.

## A New Heart for London

A short ceremony that took place below the streets of London just before Christmas in 1928 marked an important milestone for the Underground. On the morning of 10 December, the Mayor of Westminster was formally invited by Lord Ashfield to open London's latest Underground marvel by throwing a switch in the new booking hall at Piccadilly Circus station. This lit up an elaborate glass and marble Art Deco lamp and started the escalators that were about to carry thousands of passengers down to the platforms below. The mayor was issued with a 2d ticket from one of the twenty-six coin-operated ticket machines, state-of-the-art travel aids never seen in conventional railway stations at that time. He stepped on the escalator and descended under a giant painted map of the world by Stephen Bone, which homed in on London as its focal point, the busy commercial hub of the British Empire.

The Underground's showpiece development was the culmination of four years' complex engineering work at the very heart of London, where the Bakerloo and Piccadilly lines cross. Passenger numbers using Piccadilly Circus had risen from 1.5 million in 1907, after the first year's operation, to 18 million by 1922. The cramped original station could not cope with the crowds, and a major reconstruction was carried out, entirely below ground and hidden from public view. Eleven escalators replaced the original lifts, running down from a

spacious new circular entrance hall created directly below the famous road junction, and the statue of Eros was temporarily removed for its own protection while building work took place.

A large excavated space had been transformed by architect Charles Holden from a bleak engineers' hole in the ground into an attractive pedestrian concourse which became one of the sights of London. Marble wall panels, bronze fittings, glass showcases and elegant lighting made it quite unlike a traditional railway station but gave it the feel of a suitably opulent extension to the high-class shopping environment of Regent Street above. Overseas visitors were particularly impressed with this prime example of well-designed urban sophistication.

The renowned Danish urban planner Steen Eiler Rasmussen called it 'an excellent illustration of what the Underground has done for modern civilisation'. He considered it one of the finest pieces of new architecture in London, better than anything above ground. Visiting Soviet engineers preparing to build the Moscow Metro reported back to Nikita Khrushchev, their project leader, who in turn persuaded Stalin that they should use the London Underground as the model for their own planned system. Piccadilly was cited in particular, 'the best station in London, right in the heart of the most aristocratic section of the city...built deep in the ground and it has escalators rather than elevators'. In 1932 Moscow duly became the first of many world cities to use the London Underground

IMMORTALITY

PERFECTION

RIGHTEOUSNESS

WISDOM

FRANK PICK

The reconstructed station at Piccadilly was an inspired integration of the best engineering, architecture and design of the 1920s. It was commissioned by the Underground's managing director Frank Pick and perfectly demonstrates his concern that the Underground should make a positive contribution to the urban environment. A permanent memorial artwork to Pick by artists Langlands and Bell was installed in Holden's 'ambulatory' on the station concourse in 2016.

for consultancy advice on new metro construction. When the first line of the impressive Moscow Metro opened three years later Ashfield, Pick and their engineers were all awarded the Honorary Badge of the Moscow Soviet in recognition of their assistance.

## Projecting the Piccadilly

The extensions of the Hampstead and City lines in the 1920s originated from plans submitted by the Underground itself in the expectation of generating more traffic. They were not the result of outside pressure on the railway companies to provide improved services for the public. But proposals to extend the Piccadilly line originated in just this way as a result of concern by the ratepayers of north-east London at the poor and overcrowded transport facilities in the districts of the capital north of Finsbury Park.

A constant barrage of public complaints from 1919 onwards eventually persuaded the Minister of Transport to set up the London and Home Counties Transport Advisory Committee in 1925. One of the major problems on which the public inquiry concentrated was the severe rush hour congestion and potentially dangerous daily crush outside Finsbury Park station caused by the interchange between the main-line suburban trains, buses, trams and the two Tube lines which terminated here, the Great Northern & City and the Piccadilly.

Counsel for the local authorities spoke of 'pandemonium … something very like a free fight' in the evening rush hour at Finsbury Park, when commuters living further out had to change from train to bus or tram. Newspaper accounts described how 'men and women fight like rugby players to reach their homes' while 'clothes are torn, and fainting girls and women are so common as to pass almost without comment'. Whether the situation here was really any worse than at the end of other Underground lines, such as Hammersmith, is difficult to assess, but with Tube extensions already under way from Clapham and Golders Green, there was another case for projection here to take the Piccadilly line well beyond Finsbury Park. The committee report predictably recommended this so that fewer passengers would have to break their journey and continue by tram, but as usual there was no proposal over funding. It was not a priority for the Underground, which at this stage was still working on the Morden extension in south London. The main-line company operating through Finsbury Park was the LNER, which took over the GNR in 1923 and showed no more interest in its London suburban services than its predecessor.

As described in chapter 2, the GNR had prevented the Great Northern & City Tube from making a through link to its overground suburban lines here. Unlike the Southern Railway, which was busy electrifying most of its suburban

LEFT: Dangerous rush hour congestion outside Finsbury Park station, where passengers had to board trams in the middle of the road on their way home. When the Piccadilly Tube was extended in 1932 they could transfer directly from Manor House station, the next Tube stop, via subways and steps to traffic islands.

OPPOSITE: Holden made an electricity pylon the central decorative roof feature of the new station at Southgate opened in 1933.

# 55 Broadway

The rapid expansion of the Underground Electric Railways of London in the 1920s brought the need for a new company headquarters that could house the growing number of administrative and management staff and at the same time make a visual statement about the Underground's importance and progress. The success of the Morden line stations brought this prestigious architectural commission to Holden in 1926, just as he was applying a bit of panache to Piccadilly Circus. Pick, speaking at a Design and Industries Association meeting that year, promised his audience that 'a new style of architectural decoration will arise' that would herald 'Modern London – modern not garbled classic or Renaissance', almost certainly a jibe at Charles W. Clark's work for the Metropolitan at Baker Street.

55 Broadway could not have been more different from either Holden's own work at Piccadilly or Clark's at Chiltern Court. It was above ground, not below, comprised mainly offices but also included public space and housed the busy entrance and exit to St James's Park station, all on an awkward triangular site straddling the platforms. Holden saw this as an interesting challenge and found an ingenious solution in a cross-shaped plan that allowed London's first US-style skyscraper to rise up in steps above a sub-surface Underground station. He later told a meeting of civil engineers:

> I do not think I was ever more excited than when I realized the full possibilities of this cross-shaped plan – good light, short corridors and a compact centre containing all services, complete with lifts and staircases communicating directly with all four wings.

Holden achieved simplicity and grandeur at 55 Broadway, as the building has always been known, without resorting to the usual application of assorted classical add-ons favoured by most architects of office buildings at that time. The 'skyscraper' was awarded the Royal Institute of British Architects London Architectural Medal for 1929, the year it was completed. At ten storeys, it was the tallest office block in Westminster, modest by Manhattan standards but technically breaching the London County Council's building regulations. The top floor could not be used by staff until the London County Council rules were amended.

55 Broadway gained some brief public notoriety because of the sculptures on its façade. The eight artworks on the upper storeys, representing the four winds, include two by Eric Gill and the first public sculpture by the young Henry Moore. They attracted little attention, partly because they are too high up to be seen clearly from the street without binoculars. Two large sculptures representing *Day* and *Night* were carved *in situ* by Jacob Epstein at first-floor level, where they are highly visible. These dramatic avant-garde figures were heavily criticized in the popular press as being primitive, ugly and indecent. One was even attacked by vandals, who threw paint over it.

The controversy was such that Pick, who felt compelled to back his architect's judgment on this, despite his personal dislike for Epstein's work, tendered his resignation. It was not accepted. The sculptures stayed, although in a deliberately absurd gesture of compromise, Epstein dramatically chipped an inch off the penis of the naked young boy depicted in *Day*.

55 Broadway and its sculptures no longer attract special attention, but the building's fine design remains a supreme example of how to integrate an Underground station into an office development and give each equal prominence and dignity. The building, which became London Transport's head office, was listed in 1970 to give it heritage protection, although modifications to the ground-floor through route to the station entrance were permitted in the 1980s so that a reception area could be created for the offices. In 2011, English Heritage raised the building's listed status to Grade 1, which is the same top protection level as Westminster Abbey, just down the road. This recognized 55 Broadway's importance as one of the finest early twentieth-century buildings in London, and a recent proposal by Transport for London to sell the 'skyscraper' for conversion into apartments or a hotel now seems to have been abandoned.

**OPPOSITE, ABOVE: The Underground head office at 55 Broadway over St James's Park station, floodlit when newly built (left), and as a Grade 1 heritage listed building in 2018 (right).**

**OPPOSITE, BELOW: Jacob Epstein's *Night* (left) and *Day* (right) sculptures, carved *in situ* at 55 Broadway in 1928. Controversial and physically attacked at the time, the Portland stone figures are hardly noticed today and in need of a clean-up.**

lines south of the river, the LNER still avoided committing to any modernization of its suburban lines in north London in the 1920s. It was not supportive of any Underground extensions which might compete with its own overground steam services, but also claimed it could not afford to electrify. The LNER concentrated instead on its freight services, in those days more profitable than commuters, and on promoting its glamorous long-distance main-line express trains.

The Underground duly prepared a Piccadilly extension scheme but took no action until a source of capital was available. This came suddenly in 1929 when the newly elected Labour government rushed through the Development (Loans, Guarantee and Grants) Act. Like the 1921 legislation that had enabled the Edgware and Morden extensions to go ahead, this was intended to assist new works that could relieve the growing levels of unemployment, soon to get worse with the international ripple effect of the Wall Street crash. This time the government assistance on offer was broader, with fifteen-year Treasury guarantees on the interest incurred on capital loans. The theory was that by this time the extended Piccadilly would be paying its way, with healthily rising passenger revenue from new season-ticket holders in the suburbs, and the loans would be repaid. In practice, of course, like nearly all major infrastructure project repayments, this never happened.

Taking immediate advantage of the Act's generous

provision, the Underground quickly put forward a £12.4 million development programme covering far more than a northern extension to the Piccadilly line. As well as the 12 km (7½ mile) projection of the Piccadilly line from Finsbury Park through Southgate to Cockfosters, this included a 7.25 km (4½ mile) western extension overground alongside the District line, with four tracking from Hammersmith to Northfields. New Piccadilly Tube trains would then run further west over the District line branches beyond Acton Town to Hounslow and, via South Harrow, on the Uxbridge branch shared with the Metropolitan which it joined at Rayners Lane. Various major infrastructure improvements to the central area, including a new interchange station with the Central line at Holborn, were also included. The scale of the work was similar to the Northern line improvements of 1924–6.

Work began in 1930, and by 1932 the first part of the Piccadilly extensions at both the northern and western ends of the line were opened, with final completion in 1933. Again, the speed of construction was remarkable. North of Finsbury Park the line was built in twin Tube tunnels under the already built-up districts of Turnpike Lane, Wood Green and Bounds Green, coming to the surface at Arnos Grove. The line then continued overground, mainly on embankments and viaducts, through open country to rural Cockfosters, with a short tunnel under Southgate, the only village in this peaceful part of Middlesex

LEFT: Bronze-framed enamel signage, the Johnston typeface and biscuit-coloured tiling: all characteristic features of the Underground and London Transport's corporate identity in the 1930s.

RIGHT: Control panels from the electricity sub-station at Wood Green, where power from Lots Road was distributed to points on the Piccadilly line extension.

Sunrise at Southgate, where Holden created a sleek transport interchange between Tube and bus with built-in shopping facilities. Its very modern design was a complete contrast to the old village centre it invaded in 1933, but is still the perfect foil to its suburban environment.

LEFT, ABOVE: Arnos Grove
station, 1932, showing Holden
and Pick's enthusiasm for modern
Scandinavian design. This follows
the 'drum on a box' appearance
of Erik Asplund's city library in
Stockholm, completed in 1927.

LEFT, BELOW: South Harrow station,
1935, a complete environment in
the suburbs shaped by London
Transport. The bus, buildings,
signage, posters and map all reflect
the distinctive corporate identity
Pick had commissioned.

OPPOSITE: Speeding suburban
access to the West End on the new
Piccadilly line extensions, 1932.

that was still ripe for suburban development. The western extension from Hammersmith was all above ground and mainly involved widening part of the District line to four tracking and rebuilding a number of stations, including Chiswick Park and Acton Town. Depots for a new fleet of Piccadilly Tube trains with new facilities such as automated train washers were built at Cockfosters and Northfields.

In preparing its package of improvements to the Piccadilly the Underground was not simply hoping to encourage suburban development, and therefore traffic, from the outer extensions of the line. It was also trying to meet a growing market for easier and faster travel to London's West End. Throughout the Victorian period, and still to some extent in the early 1900s, the City had always been seen as the prime destination for new railway services in London. By the 1920s the West End offered a much wider range of attractions and reasons to travel than the business and financial services of the square mile. The impressive reconstruction of Piccadilly Circus station in 1924–8 as a new transport hub was the Underground's first response to this, but it only highlighted the inadequate provision elsewhere in central London.

As a result the improvement scheme also included the reconstruction of various other busy central stations such as Leicester Square as well as the closure of some inner Piccadilly line stations that were under-used. These changes, together with the additional express tracks on the Hammersmith–Acton Town section, a feature copied from the New York Subway, all contributed to the transformation of the Piccadilly into a modern rapid transit line with faster services over a route that was more than double its original length.

## A Distinctive Style

Frank Pick was as determined as ever that the new works on the Piccadilly line should follow the theory of continuous business improvement within the resources available, as well as the DIA's 'fitness for purpose' design principles that he championed. Charles Holden was retained as consulting architect to the Underground, and before work started on the new Piccadilly stations, he and Pick went on an architectural study tour of northern Europe together in 1930. They visited Germany, Scandinavia and the Netherlands to take a closer look at some of the recent commercial and civic architecture on the Continent they particularly admired. This included the work of Erik Asplund in Stockholm and Willem Dudok in the Dutch city of Hilversum. Both these architects' design styles and lean combination of brick, concrete and metal-framed glass were particularly influential on Holden's next commissioned work for the Underground.

The prototype for the Piccadilly line stations was completed at Sudbury Town in the western suburbs in July

# PICCADILLY LINE EXTENSIONS THROUGH TRAINS TO THE WEST END

| Station | Journey Time |
|---|---|
| ENFIELD WEST | **30 mins.** |
| SOUTHGATE | 28 mins. |
| ARNOS GROVE | 25 mins. |
| BOUNDS GREEN | 23 mins. |
| WOOD GREEN | 20 mins. |
| TURNPIKE LANE | 19 mins. |
| MANOR HOUSE | 16 mins. |
| FINSBURY PARK | 14 mins. |

**PICCADILLY**

| Station | Journey Time |
|---|---|
| HAMMERSMITH | 14 mins. |
| ACTON TOWN | 20 mins. |

| Station | Time | Time | Station |
|---|---|---|---|
| EALING COMMON | 21 mins. | 23 mins. | NORTHFIELDS |
| NORTH EALING | 23 mins. | | |
| PARK ROYAL | 25 mins. | | |
| ALPERTON | 28 mins. | 27 mins. | OSTERLEY |
| SUDBURY TOWN | **30 mins.** | | |
| SUDBURY HILL | 32 mins. | **30 mins.** | HOUNSLOW CENT. |
| SOUTH HARROW | 34 mins. | 32 mins. | HOUNSLOW WEST |

JOURNEY TIMES TO PICCADILLY

OPEN MAY 1932
OPEN JUNE 1932
OPEN OCT. 1932

UNDERGROUND

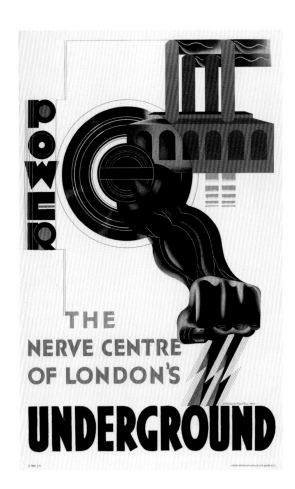

POWER

THE
NERVE CENTRE
OF LONDON'S
UNDERGROUND

THANKS TO THE

UNDERGROUND

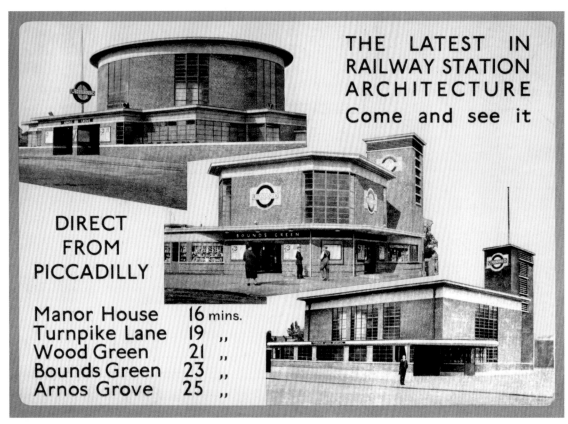

THE LATEST IN
RAILWAY STATION
ARCHITECTURE
Come and see it

DIRECT
FROM
PICCADILLY

| | | |
|---|---|---|
| Manor House | 16 | mins. |
| Turnpike Lane | 19 | ,, |
| Wood Green | 21 | ,, |
| Bounds Green | 23 | ,, |
| Arnos Grove | 25 | ,, |

OPPOSITE, ABOVE: Modernist Underground posters by Edward McKnight Kauffer (left) and 'Zero' Hans Schleger (right) in the early 1930s.

OPPOSITE, BELOW: London Underground took the unusual step of promoting its own new suburban stations on panel posters inside trains on the Piccadilly line extensions. Holden's 'brick boxes with concrete lids' were all similar but never identical.

RIGHT: Johnston's original 'pecked' lettering style for station roundels has been reinstated all over London since the 1990s. This is the flagpost style at Acton Town.

1931. It was the first of what Holden came to describe as his 'brick boxes with concrete lids'. If that sounds uninspiring, the reality is far from it. The box is double height, with four large windows arranged symmetrically above the entrance, rising to the name frieze below the cornice. The arrangement of the station was planned to stand out in a rather bland suburban landscape, but also to promote the most efficient movement of people. A generously spaced ticket hall at the main entrance gives direct access to the London-bound platform, and a covered concrete overbridge to the other.

Sudbury Town represented an even more extraordinary leap forward in station design in the United Kingdom than the Morden line. Again, it was quite unlike anything on the main-line railways or the Metropolitan. It also heralded a new era in Underground architecture. Holden's clean, simple and functional design blended traditional building forms and materials like brickwork with the modernity of concrete and careful attention to details like light fittings.

Pick, who had taken a close interest in the station's evolution, was delighted with the result but dismayed to find that fittings and equipment such as automatic vending machines had been 'dumped down and are now going to spoil the cleanness and clearness of the platforms'. He asked the operating manager to provide Holden with a complete list of all additional items to be accommodated on the stations and gave

the architect final responsibility for housing them. Holden then either designed or selected everything from seats and ticket machines to clocks and litter bins, and determined their final position. It was total design with a vengeance, an integrated approach to planning and quality standards which is still rarely followed in public buildings and environments.

Pick had set out clearly his intentions in commissioning new stations in a lecture to a group of architects in March 1930, just before the Piccadilly line work began: 'the passenger must be made to feel as though he were a guest. The doors are to be set wide open, to be modest not vast ... the sense of orderliness must flow from some unity that binds together all the various components that constitute the well-equipped station into the expression of a single idea'.

It was in this period that Pick and Holden refined the elements of what developed into an instantly recognizable Underground house style, incorporating Johnston's lettering and roundel for signs and communication. It would soon be extended to bus stops, shelters and garages to reflect the wider corporate identity of what became London Transport. The brick box at Sudbury Town established a kit of parts and materials that was reflected in new infrastructure all down the extended Piccadilly line both above and below ground, and in everything from passenger environments in stations to signal cabins, car depots and electricity sub-stations.

# The West-End is awakening—
And once again there is
everything for your pleasure

By

No two stations were exactly the same, and Holden's strong overall design identity allowed for both consistency and variation at a wide range of locations. The 'brick box' might have a drum on top of it (Arnos Grove) , become a low circular structure (Southgate), have a tower to mark it out at a distance (Chiswick Park and Osterley) or a concrete and glass trainshed to announce the end of the line (Cockfosters and Uxbridge). All the stations were recognizably 'on the Tube' and instantly made any nearby main-line suburban stations, which all dated from before 1900, look old-fashioned and shabby.

Even the new stations on the Metropolitan Railway's last extension, the branch from Wembley Park to Stanmore, which opened in December 1932, were not in the same league. These were Charles W. Clark's final works, competent but architecturally undistinguished. Holden's Piccadilly line stations included his best individual buildings, probably Arnos Grove and Southgate, and were hailed at the time as some of the finest new commercial architecture in the country. The Underground even advertised 'the latest in railway architecture' with panel posters inside the trains, encouraging passengers to 'come and see it'. No other railway company had promoted the quality of its own infrastructure in this way. Today they are nearly all heritage listed and most of them have recently been refurbished, remaining as functional and fit for purpose as any of the Underground's travel environments.

## Creating London Transport

As early as 1863, the year that the world's first underground railway had opened in London, a committee of the House of Lords had suggested that a single transport authority was needed to coordinate and integrate transport services in the capital. Over the next fifty years many government bodies had reinforced that opinion, and yet by 1913 only a limited degree of amalgamation had taken place, with none of it driven by state intervention.

The Underground Group of companies was still the most powerful force in London's public transport in the 1920s, but not in overall control. The continuing conflict of interest between the various private and municipal transport operators, particularly on the roads, with so many separate bus and tram companies, made progress with coordination particularly slow. Clearly the needs of the travelling public and London as a whole were still not being met.

Eventually the two largest operators, the Underground Group and the LCC Tramways, agreed in 1928 to promote two separate bills in parliament which would enable full coordination and joint management of their services with a common fund of earnings. Ownership would remain separate. But while these bills were going through Parliament there was a general election, in May 1929. The Labour Party, which opposed a scheme that seemed to favour the privately

OPPOSITE: Using the Tube for leisure services really took off in the 1930s, encouraged by stylish promotions like Ernest Dinkel's depiction of the West End's thriving nightlife in 1931.

RIGHT: 'New Works' by Thomas Lightfoot, 1932. It captures perfectly the progressive and ever-improving Underground image that Pick always tried to promote.

For both termini of the Piccadilly line extensions, Holden designed airy trainsheds, in modern concrete and glass, for suburban Cockfosters (1933) and five years later for Uxbridge (1938), pictured here.

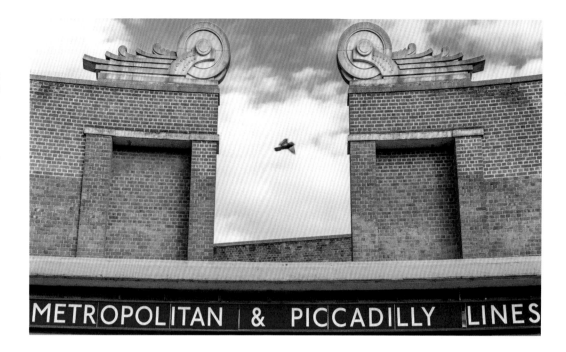

OPPOSITE, ABOVE: Stained-glass rooflights at Uxbridge by Hungarian designer Ervin Bossányi.

OPPOSITE, BELOW: Holden's elegant bronze uplighters only survive today on two station escalators, this one at Southgate (1932) and another at St John's Wood (1939). After the war, fluorescent strip lighting was introduced across the Underground. It was brighter and longer-lasting, but had no artistic style.

RIGHT: Sculpted train wheels and springs by Joseph Armitage over the entrance façade to Uxbridge station, 1938.

run UERL over the council operator, was now in control at Westminster. Both coordination bills were quickly thrown out.

However, a way forward now emerged largely through the unlikely cooperation of Lord Ashfield, the Underground Group chairman, and Herbert Morrison, the new Labour Minister of Transport. Morrison, the cockney socialist who had started his political career as a Labour member of the LCC at County Hall, had long argued against what he saw as Ashfield's ambition to create a protected, private monopoly of public transport in London. 'Common theft' was Morrison's description of it, 'a capitalist counter-offensive against public property'. Morrison wanted public ownership and control. Ashfield and Pick had consistently called for common management but did not want political interference.

In December 1929 Morrison announced his proposals for a comprehensive solution to the apparently insoluble 'London traffic problem'. At the time he seemed to be the only politician who fully understood the issues at stake and had the ability to negotiate and steer through a workable scheme that could satisfy nearly everyone. Above all, he had to get the cooperation and support of the two key industry players, Ashfield and Pick, that 'formidable pair' as he later described them. Despite their virtually opposite approach to his own, Morrison felt he could do business with them and come up with something the Underground Group would accept.

Morrison recommended the creation of a new transport board for London to be run on similar lines to the recently established BBC and Central Electricity Board. It was to be financially self-supporting and unsubsidized, with a degree of public control but non-political management. The only major element of public transport in the capital excluded from the proposed authority was the overground suburban railway network. The 'big four' main-line companies argued that their suburban services could not be run separately from their main lines, but they did eventually agree to a fare-pooling scheme in London and a joint committee with the new authority to plan future developments.

No such compromise was offered to the independent bus operators or the Metropolitan Railway, who remained firmly opposed to the scheme. The sudden death of Selbie in 1930 removed the strongest advocate of an independent Met, but the case for continuing to support the status quo was weak. Despite an active campaign against it and the fall of the Labour government in 1931, when Morrison was removed from office, the legislation was eventually passed by Parliament. On 1 July 1933 the new authority came into being. Its full title was the London Passenger Transport Board (LPTB), soon generally known as London Transport, the name that appeared in gold Johnston lettering on every bus, tram, trolleybus and Underground train in London from 1934.

# The Beck Map

The classic diagrammatic Underground map designed by Harry Beck was first produced in 1933 and became an instant success with the travelling public. It is now rightly seen as a radical breakthrough in the design of communication graphics, but often wrongly attributed to the culture of modernism that Pick had established at the Underground. Unlike Johnston's letterface and the redesign of the symbol, which had been directly commissioned by Pick himself, the new map was devised by Beck in his spare time and taken to the Underground's publicity department by him as a personal proposal. It was one individual's smart idea that met with little initial enthusiasm in the organization.

Beck was a young engineering draughtsman, who worked initially in the Underground signal engineers' office from 1925. While temporarily laid off during the Great Depression in 1931, he devised the first version of his map, apparently inspired by electrical circuit diagrams.

Every development and variation of the system map drawn up annually since 1908, when the first free pocket versions were issued, was a geographical representation of the network. Beck realized that passengers did not need a geographically accurate map, but might prefer a simple diagram showing them the sequence of stations and where to change lines to reach their destination. His line diagram abandoned geographical accuracy and all other geographical features, except the River Thames. By expanding the central area of London and shrinking the outer areas, he made the distances between stations more or less equal. The whole network is shown as a series of colour-coded interconnecting vertical, horizontal and diagonal lines.

The result is a complete distortion of London, the River Thames and the London Underground system, but as a travel aid it is brilliantly simple, being very easy to read and use. Beck pestered the publicity office for two years to get a trial run of his map, and eventually 750,000 copies were printed in January 1933, with a polite request for comments from passengers on the cover. Much to the Underground's surprise, the public reception was extremely enthusiastic.

Beck, by this time a member of staff again and working in the publicity office, was paid a derisory ten guineas (£10.50) for his initial design preparation but remained a contracted freelance for his map work. The public response to his innovative design led the Underground to make his diagram the standard system map. It has been used almost continuously since 1933, with regular changes and additions, both as a large poster map displayed in station ticket halls and on platforms and as a free folding pocket map for travellers.

Beck had a difficult relationship with London Transport for the rest of his working life. He insisted on retaining control of the map and personally overseeing all changes himself for more than twenty-five years, even after he left London Transport employment in the late 1940s. His constant revisions and meticulous reworkings became almost an obsession, and inevitably there were frequent clashes with the publicity office until a final falling out took place. The last map with his name on it was printed in 1959.

Beck died in 1974, bitter to the end at what he felt had been his unreasonable treatment by London Transport, particularly in the 1960s when he was neither involved in further exchanges nor acknowledged as the map's originator. Eventually, by the 1990s, the significance of his enormous contribution to graphic design development through the map became widely recognized. His name reappeared under the large-format system maps on every London Underground station, and the map itself became an icon of modernism, endlessly copied, imitated and plagiarized in advertising and artworks.

The greatest tribute to Beck's map is not in the various imitations and copies elsewhere, but in its astonishing versatility and adaptability as a travel guide to London. This flexibility has allowed a multitude of extensions and additions to be fitted into its grid over the years, although the pocket Tube map has probably now reached its limit of legibility with the incorporation of the DLR, Tramlink, London Overground and Elizabeth line networks. When the Battersea branch of the Northern line is squeezed in from 2020, this will surely be the last addition.

Despite its denial of the city's true geography, the Tube map's alternative vision of the city has become a familiar feature of London life that few people would wish to see changed. In 2006, it came second in a BBC competition to find the public's favourite British design of the twentieth century, beaten only by Concorde. When Beck's distorted and angular River Thames disappeared from the pocket map in 2009, there was uproar on the web and in the media. The mayor was forced to step in and guarantee the river's reinstatement for the next edition. Popular outrage might make any more fundamental redesign of this London icon an impossible challenge.

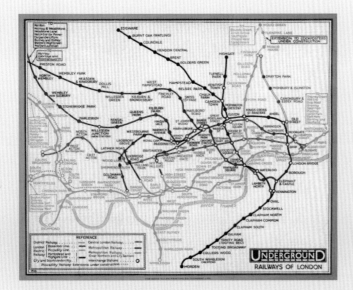

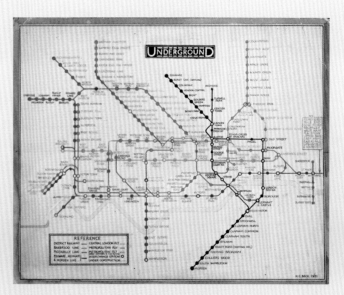

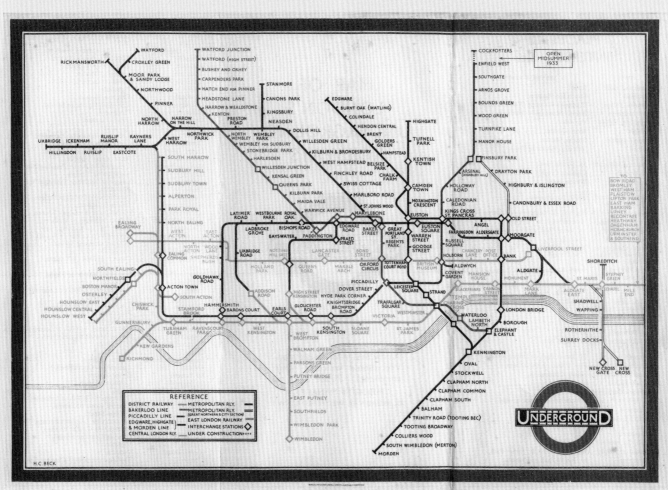

TOP, LEFT: The 1931 edition of the pocket Tube map, designed by Fred Stingemore.

TOP, RIGHT: Harry Beck's first presentation design, offered to the Underground in 1931 and initially rejected.

ABOVE: The first printed Beck diagrammatic pocket map, 1933. A polite notice on the cover read 'A new design for an old map. We should welcome your comments.'

Under the LPTB, ultimate authority was removed from the various local authorities that had run council tram services and from the shareholders of all the London bus, tram and underground railway companies, from the pirates to the Combine. All shareholders received either cash payments or shares in the new undertaking. There was some public control over new developments but real power rested with the Board, which in practice was dominated by the leading individuals and inherited management practice of the Underground Group. Lord Ashfield became the LPTB's first chairman and Frank Pick the vice chairman and chief executive.

The London Traffic Area for which the LPTB was responsible was much larger than the current boundaries of Greater London, which is roughly the M25 ring, or an area 24–32 km (15–20 miles) from central London. From 1933 London Transport covered some 5,175 km² (2,000 square miles) within a 32–48 km (20–30 mile) radius of Charing Cross, including a large area of London's countryside, which was served by green country buses and Green Line coaches. London Transport had to plan and provide public road and rail services for a population then approaching 9.5 million people.

## New Works Programme

Ashfield and Pick had always been clear that a metropolis of London's size and complexity needed a suitable mix of public transport provision in different areas: buses, trams, underground and overground railways. The problem they had faced throughout the 1920s had been the absence of co-ordination between these modes, caused largely by the range of ownership and management. This had made effective forward planning difficult if not impossible, because their UERL did not have complete control of any one area or mode of transport, although it had a partial involvement in all of them.

The creation of the LPTB changed this situation at a stroke, as it effectively gave the new organization a virtual monopoly, but it also brought with it new obligations and expectations. As chairman and chief executive of a public corporation, Ashfield and Pick now had responsibilities which were no less demanding than those to the UERL's former private shareholders. London Transport was a public service authority on an unprecedented scale, with a formidable challenge ahead of it.

A continuing difficulty was how to break even financially. This inevitably required a degree of cross-subsidy within the LPTB between its road and rail services. Buses were still profitable, earning more from fares than they cost to run, but could not cope with London's travel needs on their own. The large London tram network now carried fewer passengers than the buses and was losing money. Major renewals or complete replacement of the system were necessary.

LEFT: Passengers on the new escalators at Holborn, 1935. Similar uplighters were adopted for the new Moscow Metro, which opened its first line that year after taking consultancy advice from London Underground. Pick, Ashfield and their senior engineers were all awarded the Honorary Badge of the Moscow Soviet in recognition of their help.

OPPOSITE: Rayners Lane station, rebuilt by Leonard Bucknell under the supervision of Charles Holden for London Transport in 1938, to cope with the rapid expansion of commuting from the new Metro-land suburb.

Variations on Holden's 'brick box with a concrete lid' architectural style for the Underground in the 1930s at Chiswick Park (above and below), Acton Town (left) and St John's Wood (opposite).

The Underground was now the essential transport network underpinning London which required further investment, but it was also expensive to run. In 1933 the LPTB inherited an underground railway network covering 227 route miles and carrying some 415 million passengers a year. Both needed to grow. As Pick put it at a senior staff conference in 1937:

> The railways represent an inescapable basic service for London. Whether they are able to operate at an efficiency which makes them financially sound or not, they must be provided to support the mass of road transport that has been built up around them. They have every claim to a subsidy from road transport if that be the only basis upon which they can be enlarged and continued.

London Transport's ambitious plans in the 1930s involved modernizing and developing services, vehicles and infrastructure across the board. On the roads it was decided that all new buses should have more efficient diesel instead of petrol engines. Trams would be replaced by electric trolleybuses, which were cheaper and more flexible to run because they did not require special trackwork in the road but could continue to use the existing electrical power distribution network of the trams. More than half of London's huge tram

network was replaced by trolleybuses in this way between 1935 and 1940.

The flexible but distinctive corporate design style that Pick and Holden had established together for the Piccadilly line extensions was now developed and expanded across all the LPTB's road and rail facilities, from bus garages to street shelters. Holden himself became preoccupied with a commission to design a large new campus for the University of London in Bloomsbury, starting with the Senate House complex behind the British Museum. His small architectural practice could not possibly have handled all the new work coming from London Transport, and having established a new framework much of the supervision was entrusted to other consulting architects or the LPTB's in-house team under Stanley Heaps.

Pick, as an obsessive details man, was not happy with this delegation but eventually recognized its inevitability. Compromises were made, but overall the stylish and understated look of London Transport after 1933 followed on seamlessly from the design format established by Holden for the UERL's Piccadilly line. It was not diluted, but often enhanced by collaboration with other architects in the final design of new stations such as Rayners Lane (1936), Uxbridge (1938) and East Finchley (1939), all with Leonard Bucknell. Some had no involvement from Holden at all but retain elements

London Transport Museum's four-car 1938 Tube stock set on a special heritage service in 2018. It was then eighty years old but restored to full working order as the 'Art Deco Tube train'. This is Ealing Common station, another Holden design of 1931, carried out with the Underground's in-house architect. 1938 stock trains are still in service on the Isle of Wight, where they are used on the Island Line between Ryde Pierhead and Shanklin.

of his distinctive, established house style for the LPTB: for example Park Royal by Welch & Lander (1936), West Acton by GWR architect Brian Lewis, (1940) and Loughton by John Murray Easton for the LNER (also 1940, but not used by Tube trains until 1947).

The first in a series of new Underground infrastructure schemes for the LPTB was announced in November 1934, involving upgrades to the Metropolitan line. A new branch of the Bakerloo Tube would run below the Met between Baker Street and Finchley Road, relieving overcrowding on this section. There was to be cross-platform interchange at Finchley Road and Bakerloo services would be projected overground alongside the Met to Wembley Park, taking over the newly built branch to Stanmore.

As part of London Transport, the Met was no longer permitted the luxury of regarding itself as a main-line railway, and operations at the outer end of the line beyond Aylesbury in rural Bucks were soon cut back. The lightly used Brill branch, which wandered off the main line at Quainton Road and was worked by sixty-year-old Met steam locomotives with a mixed goods and passenger train, was finally closed in 1935. Two years later the LNER took over the remaining steam passenger workings beyond the outer limit of electrification at Rickmansworth, and London Transport transferred half of their inherited Metropolitan Railway steam engines to the main-line company.

The LNER also took over the remaining goods and parcels services of the Met, a final recognition that this was no longer part of the core business of a modern, urban passenger railway. Pick also quickly banished the name Metro-land from the LPTB's publicity programme and severed all links with Metropolitan Railway Country Estates Ltd, the housing and property company Selbie had set up. By the 1930s Pick had become more concerned with managing the spread of suburbia and containing London's inexorable outward expansion with a Green Belt. He even appeared to question the legality of Selbie's direct involvement in private housing provision and seemed like the classic poacher turned gamekeeper now that suburban development seemed to be getting out of control.

London Transport's wider 1935–40 New Works Programme for the Underground was planned in partnership with the LNER and GWR, to further improve suburban services in north, east and west London, all with government-guaranteed loans. The Central line was to be extended in the west on new surface tracks from North Acton to Ruislip and Denham. An eastern extension would run in Tube tunnels from Liverpool Street to Stratford, where it would come to the surface before joining up with one of the LNER's branch lines into Essex. The existing steam suburban services from Liverpool Street to Epping, Ongar and the Hainault loop line, linked by new Tube tunnels under the Eastern Avenue to serve the heavily populated areas

# The World's Best Trains

The new underground trains developed by London Transport in the 1930s were unquestionably the best in the world. The UERL's business philosophy of continuous improvement meant that engineering research and design development had become increasingly sophisticated since the creation of Acton railway works in west London in 1921–2, built alongside the London General Omnibus Company's Chiswick bus works, which was constructed at the same time. The growing complex at Acton housed the Underground's main overhaul and repair facilities, which were centralized and run on the latest factory 'flow line' principles adopted from the United States. The UERL's new rolling stock was not built at Acton, but all train design, development and experimental work took place there.

US-born William S. Graff-Baker, who became the LPTB's chief mechanical engineer (railways) in 1935, had worked for the Underground since joining as a junior electrical fitter in 1910. He led the team that designed the advanced new Tube and sub-surface trains that entered service from 1937 to 1938 as part of the New Works Programme, and he was also responsible for lift and escalator development.

The small diameter of London's deep-level tunnels limited the size of Tube trains, and Graff-Baker's engineers experimented with new space-saving techniques. The control equipment, which took up about 25 per cent of each driving motor car behind the cab of the standard Tube stock built from 1923 to 1934, was ingeniously redistributed and located below the floor of experimental cars built in 1935, thereby giving more room for passenger seating.

The interior design and layout were improved, with new flexible grab handles for 'straphangers' and deep-cushioned seating, now covered in woollen moquette fabric specially commissioned from textile designers rather than chosen from the manufacturers' standard range. Christian Barman, the LPTB's newly appointed publicity officer, selected independent artist designers such as Enid Marx, Marion Dorn and Paul Nash to come up with new ideas for industrial production. The new Tube cars still had varnished, slatted hardwood floors, which, combined with the red and green panels and seating units, had a warm and inviting appearance. Everything was highly functional but looked surprisingly luxurious, right down to the Art Deco glass lampshades.

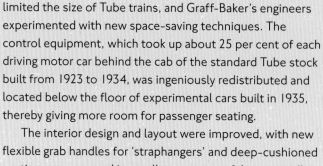

**W.S. Graff-Baker (left), who became the LPTB's Chief Mechanical Engineer (Railways) in 1935 and led on the design of all new trains, including the flare-sided surface stock introduced in 1937 (below left) and the experimental streamlined Tube stock trialled in 1935/6 (right) which was soon succeeded by the flat-fronted 1938 Tube stock (below right).**

Trials with fully streamlined Tube cars demonstrated that this fashionable 1930s body styling was of little benefit to low-speed trains in close-fitting tunnels. However, the smooth exterior finish of the new prototype cars, with uncluttered body panels and flush-fitted windows, was adopted for mass production. This was not only a more attractive design but was also of practical benefit when trains were being cleaned in the new automatic washing machines at depots. In addition, passengers could open the pneumatic doors with push buttons and the driver could now talk directly to the guard at the back of the train through a speaking tube. A new 'wedglock' automatic coupler made it easier and quicker to lengthen or shorten trains as required.

All these improved features were incorporated in the production of 1938 stock built for the LPTB in Birmingham, which is now regarded as the classic London Tube train design. It did not have the glamour of the famous streamlined steam express trains of the period, such as the *Silver Jubilee* and *Coronation Scot*, but it was a technically far more advanced and sophisticated design.

Graff-Baker took a similar view to Pick and Holden on the crucial importance of good, practical design and engineering. In his presidential address to the Locomotive and Carriage Institution in October 1938, he set out the five key questions that should be asked of any new development in train design: Will it work? Is it as simple as possible? Could it easily be maintained in service? Can it be manufactured? Does it look good?

'Engineering design', he claimed, 'is an art just as much as is the work of a painter or an architect.' Some of his beautifully designed pieces of applied art were in service on the London Underground for fifty years and a four-car set of 1938 stock has been restored to working order by London Transport Museum for occasional public outings.

The warm colours and attractive styling of 1938 stock, which set a template for London Transport Tube trains until the 1960s.

of North Ilford, would all be taken over by electric Tube trains running right into the City and West End on the Central line.

London Transport would also take over and electrify the LNER's 'Northern Heights' suburban branch lines with new links to the Northern line. An extension from the original 1907 Tube terminus at Highgate (Archway) would come to the surface at East Finchley and join the existing LNER line to High Barnet. Tube trains would take over from steam on the overground sections, which would be electrified back to Finsbury Park and finally make the connection with the Great Northern & City line to Moorgate. The Highgate to Alexandra Palace and Finchley Church End to Edgware branches would all become part of the Northern line network, with a further northern extension beyond Edgware to Bushey Heath. All of this would relieve the LNER of some of the suburban commuter services it could not afford to electrify and which clogged up the constricted approaches to its London termini at King's Cross and Liverpool Street.

This added up to a massive series of capital projects which included extensive modernization and improvement works to the existing Central line in particular, which had not been built to the same standard as the later UERL Tubes. The original Central London three rail electrification system would at last be made compatible, as the C&SLR had been in the 1920s, with the four-rail American standard of the UERL lines. This meant

complete track replacement, enlarging tunnels, improved signalling and rebuilding key stations in preparation for the introduction of new trains in place of the antiquated original CLR stock which was nearly forty years old.

London Transport's New Works Programme was to be financed by the now well-established mechanism of loans under government guarantee. No public money was granted, but this time Treasury agreement was given for a finance corporation to be created which would raise the £40 million required for the whole package. Government support through guarantees of interest on loans enabled finance to be raised at a lower rate of interest than would have been available by a direct approach to the market (2.5 per cent instead of about 3.75 per cent, a substantial saving).

Work began on all three Tube lines involved (Bakerloo, Central and Northern lines) in 1936 and proceeded rapidly. London Transport had inherited the UERL's skills and experience in managing large engineering and infrastructure projects. For Ashfield and Pick the greater worry was maintaining revenue funding and their obligation to cover the LPTB's running costs. The financial viability of both the Underground's existing operations and planned future development depended on the continued growth and expansion of London attracting yet more passengers on to the system. Reviewing their performance after five years, the Board wrote in 1938 of their 'conflict of duty',

LEFT: The tunnel mouth where the Northern line came to the surface at East Finchley in 1938 before joining the LNER steam branch to High Barnet.

OPPOSITE, ABOVE AND BELOW: St John's Wood Tube station on the new branch of the Bakerloo line, designed by Stanley Heaps in the Holden style and opened in November 1939. Forty years later this was transferred to form part of the new Jubilee line.

both to maintain financial stability and to improve and develop facilities. It was almost impossible to satisfy both objectives. They suggested that 'in every way the passenger must recognize that much has been accomplished on his behalf even if he may feel on occasion unsatisfied'.

Taxation and general prices kept rising in the 1930s, with working expenses increasing faster than traffic receipts. While operation was becoming ever more efficient, the most recent extensions of the Piccadilly line and the Metroplitan's Stanmore branch were not providing as much extra traffic as had been hoped and planned for. New suburban housing followed both lines, but more slowly than at Hendon and Edgware in the international downturn that followed the Wall Street crash of 1929. London and the south-east were less seriously affected by economic depression than the industrial north but recovery took time.

Londoners were also not used to price rises on public transport in peacetime, although they had accepted it as a temporary phenomenon during the First World War. The LPTB was very reluctant to go beyond the broadly accepted 'penny a mile' basis for fares, but in 1939 it was driven to get its first approval for a general fare increase from the Railway Rates Tribunal.

London Transport's rapid progress in modernization and improvement was remarkable, yet by 1938 it was being slowed by new financial uncertainty and the deteriorating international situation in Europe following the Nazis' accession to power in Germany. The eventual outbreak of war in September 1939 stopped London's suburban sprawl in its tracks. Of London Transport's development programme, only the Bakerloo extension was almost complete. A new Tube service from Stanmore through to the West End opened in November. From April 1940 Northern line Tube trains were running right up to High Barnet over the LNER's former steam branch line. But by this time all other New Works projects had been suspended for the duration of the war, some never to be completed. The Blitz was about to begin and London Transport's brief boom years, now subject to severe financial and resource constraints, were suddenly over.

OPPOSITE: 'More for You' poster announcing through-trains from High Barnet on the newly electrified surface section of the Northern line, April 1940. All further planned new works were then suspended until the end of the war, most of them on the Northern line never to be completed.

## ◯ The Idea of a Railway Station

In the process of leaving London Transport (see page 185), Pick wrote to Holden in May 1940, reflecting on their past work together on Underground design and what might happen in the future after the war:

It is indeed strange how the idea of a railway station still germinates to bring forth fresh flower and fruit. Just as you suppose you have analysed its functions and purposes completely and given them just expression, so something new springs into view and a fresh rationalization of the elements in an architectural unity is demanded. We have not yet solved for example interchange in comfort and convenience between road and rail vehicles – Morden, Edgware, Osterley, South Harrow and Uxbridge are all deficient in this sense. So I can wish you joy as soon as this war is over in another attempt to catch up with requirements and add to the monuments of London suited to this industrial age.

# 6 War and Austerity

# THE PROUD CITY

CHELSEA POWER HOUSE FROM MEEK STREET

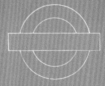

"...the poor buildings lose themselves in the dim sky, and the tall chimneys become campanili, and the warehouses are palaces in the night, and the whole city hangs in the heavens..."
James McNeill Whistler

**PREVIOUS PAGES:** Original 1906 tiled stairway and wooden handrails at Covent Garden which would have been used by passengers and shelterers during the war.

**OPPOSITE:** Wartime poster by Walter Spradbery celebrating the Blitzed city's survival, 1944. Ironically, the artist Whistler, who is quoted here, had strongly opposed the construction of Lots Road power station forty years earlier.

**LEFT:** A policewoman supervises the evacuation of London schoolchildren from the District line to the Great Western main line at Ealing Broadway on the outbreak of war, September 1939.

**ABOVE:** 'Goodbye Hitler'. A London Transport bus takes children out of the city to the country under the evacuation scheme administered by Frank Pick at the start of the war in 1939.

## The Tube Prepares for War

London Transport was far more prepared for war in 1939 than the Underground had been in August 1914. Back then, war had seemed a distant reality when it was declared, only gradually impacting on the travelling public as, against early expectation, the conflict dragged on. The employment of women on trains, trams and buses, together with food and fuel shortages, severe overcrowding and sporadic air attacks, was all part of an entirely new phenomenon, the Home Front, which was experienced by everyone. Peace came as a relief after four long years, but there was little confidence that this had been 'the war to end all wars' and that the settlement would last.

Twenty years after the Armistice, few were in doubt that another war with Germany would have a far more immediate and devastating impact. Many shared the government's pessimistic assessment that London would be disabled within days by sustained bombing raids, with civilian casualties in the tens of thousands. As early as 1932, the Conservative prime minister Stanley Baldwin had warned the British people that 'the bomber will always get through'. Five years later, the devastation caused by German war planes intervening in the Spanish Civil War showed what could happen across Europe as international tensions mounted again. Underlying these fears was the real possibility that the enemy would use poison gas to cause havoc in a large city like London.

At 11.15 a.m. on Sunday 3 September 1939, households all over Britain tuned into their wireless sets for a broadcast from the prime minister Neville Chamberlain, announcing a state of war with Germany. It came as no surprise. War with Nazi Germany as a result of Hitler's aggression towards Poland and other neighbouring countries had seemed increasingly likely for months. Exactly a year earlier, during the Munich crisis, hostilities had been averted at the last moment by Chamberlain's personal 'piece of paper' agreement with Hitler, widely seen as a futile appeasement. It soon became clear that this had only postponed the inevitable conflict.

The borrowed time had at least allowed some preparations to be made against the expected aerial bombardment by the Luftwaffe. London Transport, like most large organizations, had followed government instructions and appointed an Air Raid Precautions (ARP) committee as early as 1937. By September 1938, the London Passenger Transport Board (LPTB) had drawn up detailed defence plans that would allow London's transport system to remain operational under aerial attack, with the safety of passengers and staff secured as far as possible. The greatest single threat to the operation of the Underground was thought to be flooding from damage to the District line along the Thames Embankment and bomb penetration to the deep Bakerloo and Northern line Tubes that ran under the river nearby. Temporary concrete plugs had been installed in these tunnels during the Munich crisis, replaced by massive electrically controlled steel floodgates over the following year. These took just thirty seconds to close during an air raid and were fully operational by the time war broke out in September 1939.

Frank Pick took personal charge of the LPTB's planning. Detailed schemes were drawn up in cooperation with the London County Council (LCC) for the evacuation of London's children, hospital patients and expectant mothers. Nearly 13,000 evacuees were ferried to Waterloo by bus, tram and Tube for transfer on to main-line trains out of the city. Many more were taken to railway stations outside central London, such as Ealing Broadway and New Barnet, to relieve pressure on the main termini. Within two days and by the time war was officially declared, over 600,000 vulnerable Londoners, most of them schoolchildren, had left the capital with London Transport's assistance, an amazing triumph of logistics.

Selected staff had already received training in all branches of civil defence, including anti-gas measures, first aid and firefighting. More than 6,000 were fully qualified by 1940, rising to 20,000 by the end of the war. More than £1 million was spent on comprehensive defensive works, ranging from staff shelters and first aid posts at depots to the strengthening of bridges and the installation of anti-blast walls at station entrances. Brompton Road Tube station on the Piccadilly line,

which had been closed to passengers since 1934, was sold to the government in 1938 for military defence use. The deep-level areas were then converted to house the main ops room for London's anti-aircraft control, which was based there throughout the war.

Some other disused stations were converted at lower level into (almost) bomb-proof offices for military and government use. The onset of war brought with it immediate changes for the management and operation of London Transport, not least because the LPTB came under the direct control of a new government body, the Railway Executive Committee (REC). Day-to-day management remained in the hands of the London Passenger Transport Board (LPTB), with the REC taking a strategic role on matters affecting the coordination of the national rail network. Down Street, a lightly used central Piccadilly Tube station that had closed in 1932, was adapted for use by the REC and later the War Cabinet in 1940–41. It still retains evidence of its wartime past in the form of stencilled notices on the walls and a dingy bathroom and bedroom installed for Winston Churchill's personal use. This secret location, inaccessible to unauthorized visitors for more than seventy years, can now be seen on guided tours of the station via London Transport Museum's Hidden London programme.

Pick represented the Board on the REC, but his tenure was to be short-lived. Senior colleagues complained that

LEFT: Tube travel in the blackout, with all train windows covered in anti-splinter netting, 1942.

ABOVE: Brompton Road station on the Piccadilly line, closed in 1934, was converted to provide a secure deep-level operations room for London's anti-aircraft control.

BELOW: A permanent way gang practise rail replacement in their cumbersome anti-gas suits at Neasden depot, February 1940. Fortunately the Germans did not use gas in the Blitz raids on London that began six months later.

RIGHT: Winter sales advertised in New Year 1940 when barrage balloons were tethered over central London to discourage low-flying bomb attacks.

WINTER SALES
SPEND TO SAVE
SAVE TO LEND

CHEAP
TICKETS
TO TOWN

SHOP
BETWEEN
10 AND 4

Pick, always a difficult and demanding person to work with, had become even more distant and aloof during this stressful time, unilaterally making decisions on the LPTB's behalf without proper consultation. Ashfield was worried about Pick's mental and physical health and relieved him of some of the more mundane aspects of his job, ostensibly to allow time for recuperation, but this probably did little to assist the workaholic Pick.

Matters came to a head early in 1940 when Pick and Ashfield clashed over government terms for the financial management of the LPTB during the war. Following a stormy meeting, Pick offered his resignation, which Ashfield accepted, informing the Board that Pick was leaving due to ill health. There was clearly more to it than that, but Ashfield made no attempt to persuade Pick to stay or to extend his seven-year contract with the LPTB, which was coming to an end. It was a sad finale to their long working partnership, which had lasted for more than thirty years and had effectively both created and run the Underground Group and London Transport.

## The Shelter of the Tubes

Official government policy, announced on 3 September 1939, was that Tube stations would not be available as public air raid shelters. This was all very well during the 'phoney war' of the winter and spring of 1939–40, before there were any aerial attacks, but it was impossible to sustain once the Blitz began a year later. The provision of shelters was still woefully behind schedule and Londoners had little faith in the few poorly designed street shelters that had been built. These became known as 'concrete sandwiches', because if their brick walls were blown out in a bomb blast, the concrete roofs could collapse and crush anyone sheltering inside. In the East End, targeted by the Luftwaffe because of its docks, warehouses and industry, homes did not have basements to provide basic shelter and very few domestic gardens could house the corrugated iron Anderson shelters being distributed by local councils.

In 1917, many Londoners had flocked to the safety of the Tubes during the German aerial raids of the First World War. Underground posters advising that it was 'bomb proof down below' had even encouraged it. Memories of the Home Front in the Great War created an expectation in 1940 that sheltering in a Tube station would still be the safest option, despite the clear official ban.

London Transport continued to maintain that the greatest contribution the Underground could make to public safety would be by dispersing people home each evening, keeping the system running and not concentrating crowds in shelters that might receive a direct hit. Less publicly, the government was also concerned about the creation of a 'deep shelter mentality'

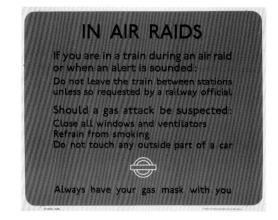

IN AIR RAIDS

If you are in a train during an air raid
or when an alert is sounded:
Do not leave the train between stations
unless so requested by a railway official

Should a gas attack be suspected:
Close all windows and ventilators
Refrain from smoking
Do not touch any outside part of a car

Always have your gas mask with you

**ABOVE:** 'In Air Raids': signage, 1940.

**LEFT:** 'A Woman's Job in War': a 1941 London Transport recruitment poster featuring Miss Maylin, a station porter at Shepherd's Bush.

**OPPOSITE:** Shelterers bedding down on the escalators at Piccadilly Circus in the early nights of the Blitz, September 1940.

and the complete collapse of public morale. If terrified Londoners refused to leave the protection of the Tube, there could be serious civil unrest and a rapid loss of essential services.

The long-expected air raids started in earnest with a heavy daylight attack on London by Luftwaffe bombers on 7 September 1940, aimed at the docks and the East End. London was then bombed every night until 2 November, after which the Blitz continued intermittently until May 1941. Everywhere, crowds rushed to use the Underground as the most reliable shelter. Station staff were helpless to resist and at Liverpool Street, the closest Tube to the East End, they just opened the gates and let the crowds in. There were similar scenes all over central London, where people simply bought the cheapest ticket to get into a station and stayed there underground when the air raid sirens went off.

The press, initially discouraged from reporting the Underground invasion, referred to the nightly Tube dwellers as 'Tubites'. London Transport called them squatters. Soon it was estimated that nearly 180,000 Londoners were occupying seventy-nine of the LPTB's deep-level stations every night, arriving from all over town. 'From Earl's Court to Leicester Square,' reported the *Evening Standard* on 27 September, 'every platform was covered with people sitting on newspapers and leaning against the wall.'

At first, nothing was organized and conditions were pretty grim. Trains continued to run until 10.30 p.m., with passengers and shelterers jostling each other on the overcrowded platforms as people arrived to stay the night. When the last train had departed and the station had closed, people bedded down wherever they could: on platforms, in passageways, even on escalators. Most shelterers stayed until the all clear was sounded in the early hours of the morning. Drinking water was in very short supply, and there were no toilet or washing facilities. As one eyewitness recalled: 'Personal hygiene rather went out of the window, but you just got used to it.'

Within a few weeks, the unenforceable ban on Tube sheltering was lifted following the prime minister's personal intervention. Churchill ordered an urgent review and a policy U-turn was announced. On 8 October, the home secretary, Herbert Morrison, told the House of Commons: 'As far as is consistent with public safety and with the overriding necessity of maintaining essential public transport facilities . . . the public are now allowed to use the Tube for shelter purposes.'

Forced into an abrupt about-face, London Transport coaxed back into service its recently retired general manager (railways), John P. Thomas, to organize a proper sheltering system on the Tube. Very quickly, a separate ticketing arrangement for sheltering rather than travelling had been introduced, linked to numbered metal bunk beds installed on the platforms at

West Acton, the only new Modernist station to be designed and built in the 1930s by the Great Western architect Brian Lewis, was opened in November 1940 when the Blitz had begun. All other planned new work on the western end of the Central line was postponed until after the war.

LEFT: Entrance to the disused Tube station on the Aldwych branch, originally opened as Strand in 1907 but only ever run as a shuttle service to Holborn using one platform and tunnel. It finally closed to passengers in 1994 but is still linked to the main Tube system and used for filming and emergency planning.

ABOVE: The short Aldwych branch was closed during the war and one tunnel was used for secure storage of museum collections. The main station area became a civilian air raid shelter run by Westminster City Council with a range of entertainment facilities such as concerts, often broadcast by the BBC.

seventy-six deep-level stations. There was still no running water at platform level, but chemical toilets were provided along with medical and first aid posts run by volunteer nurses from the Red Cross and St John's Ambulance Brigade. There was even a nightly Tube refreshments service provided by London Transport, which distributed cheap food to the shelterers (mostly tea, pies and buns) in six special trains.

Various abandoned, partly built or little used sections of the Tube were turned over to local authorities for use as public shelters. These included the original King William Street terminus of the City & South London Railway, unused since 1900, and the unfinished Central line extension tunnels beyond Liverpool Street. On the short Piccadilly branch from Holborn to Aldwych, where only one tunnel and platform were in regular use for the shuttle service, the redundant tunnel was adapted to form a secure store for museum treasures, including the Elgin marbles from the British Museum. The other tunnel and platform area at Aldwych became a civilian shelter run by Westminster City Council, which opened in October 1940. Train services on the branch were suspended for the duration, with some of the rails removed and the anti-suicide pit boarded over for the installation of bunk beds on the track area. With no passengers to deal with, Aldwych was adapted by early 1941 to provide up to 1,500 ticket-only spaces and bunk beds for civilian shelterers in addition to the separate area for museum artefacts.

Across the Underground, the number of nightly shelterers fell from a peak of 177,500 in late September to about 120,000 by Christmas 1940. With the end of the intensive period of the Blitz in May 1941, the number of regular shelterers dropped sharply to a low of about 5,000 in 1942. Even with this decline, the Tube's reputation for being the 'safest shelter of all' ensured that it continued to be used every night until the end of the war, with numbers again reaching more than 150,000 during the V1 and V2 rocket attacks of 1944–5.

Tube sheltering had become the most well-known feature of the London Blitz almost as soon as it began, especially when it was heavily publicized in newsreels, feature films and newspapers in the United States. Popular magazines in Britain, such as *Picture Post*, had dramatic picture spreads by Bill Brandt and other photographers, while the shelterers were portrayed in very different ways by artists including Edward Ardizzone and Henry Moore. As many of the nation's greatest cultural treasures from the British Museum, Tate Gallery, V&A and National Gallery were placed in underground storage in the Tube for protection, these newly created artworks depicting the shelterers were soon put on temporary display above ground in some of the denuded museum galleries.

Sheltering in the Tube was quickly transformed into a symbol of stoic civilian resistance and Blitz spirit, becoming an uplifting narrative about British resolve in a crisis. It was even featured in

ABOVE AND RIGHT: London Transport sent Tube Refreshments Special trains round the shelter stations every night, supplying teas, pies and buns to Tube shelterers who had no cooking facilities underground.

BELOW: Aldwych can now be visited on guided tours organized by the London Transport Museum. The two original Otis lifts installed in 1907 are still in place, though not operational.

# Life Underground

Some stations had shelterers committees that organized libraries, lectures and religious services and even published their own newsletters, such as the *Swiss Cottager* and the *Subway Companion*. There were also invited shows held in the Tube shelters, put on by the wartime Entertainment National Service Association, which provided popular professional entertainers such as Arthur Askey. One of these concerts, featuring George Formby with Geraldo and his orchestra, was staged on the platform at Aldwych in November 1940 and was broadcast to the United States by the BBC.

Mass Observation, the social research organization founded in 1937, reported:

> For the first time in many hundreds of years, civilized families conducted the whole of their leisure and domestic lives in full view of each other. . . . Most of these people were not merely sheltering in the Tubes, they were living there.

It was not exactly comfortable, but Mass Observation also found that some Tube dwellers were reluctant to return home even when they could, especially because living underground was cheap and relatively cheerful. For many who were bombed out of their homes, it was their only option, and a real community spirit developed between people who had been forced together by war. One pregnant woman became so attached to her subterranean home, some 30 m (98 ft) below the Strand, that she had to be ordered out of the Tube shelter and to hospital by doctors; she had wanted to give birth underground and name her baby 'Aldwych'.

**RIGHT, ABOVE AND BELOW:** Shelterers using the bunk beds installed along the platform walls at most deep Tube stations in the autumn of 1940.

**FAR RIGHT, ABOVE:** The new fully equipped civilian shelter at Clapham South, completed and opened in 1942. After the war it became temporary accommodation for West Indian migrants arriving on the *Windrush* in 1948 and a cheap hostel for young people visiting the Festival of Britain in 1951.

**FAR RIGHT, BELOW:** Trains were still running during the day at most shelter stations and London Transport had to enforce strict new rules of behaviour!

# SHELTERERS' BEDDING

The practice of shaking bedding over the platforms, tracks and in the subways is strictly forbidden

Pilot, all alone you ride
  Through the bowels of the town,
Up into the black outside
  Where the bombs are whistling down.

Bombs and blizzards, fogs and frights —
  "Dead man's handle" at your breast —
Lights — and lights — for ever lights —
  On you ride and never rest.

On to Barking, on to Kew!
  Master of a trying trade,
Seldom do we think of you,
  Never do we feel afraid.

A. P. Herbert

a widely shown Ministry of Information newsreel titled *A Tale of Two Cities* alongside the Russian defence of Moscow, where civilians sheltered in their own Metro during the German invasion of the Soviet Union. This was positive propaganda, which Joseph Goebbels could never match for Hitler and the Nazis.

As the *Evening Standard* reported when the last bunk beds were removed from the Tube platforms in 1945:

> So ended one of the most extraordinary chapters in all London's history. It is a strange story: a story of how a body of London citizens, ignoring flustered authority and obeying their own common sense, saved themselves and their children from the enemy assault.

## Surviving the Crisis

Even the deep Tube tunnels were not entirely safe from bombing, and nearly 200 people were killed when Tube shelters received direct hits. The worst incident in terms of casualties among shelterers took place at Balham on 14 October 1940, when a bomb pierced the High Road, fracturing pipes and water mains. Mud and sewage flooded the station platforms far below, and sixty-four shelterers died, together with four members of the station staff. Above ground, the crew of a double-decker bus that was blown into the bomb crater were miraculously unscathed. It took two months to repair the damage to the

road and the station below. A memorial plaque to those who lost their lives can be seen today at the station entrance.

Similar plaques can be seen on the platform at Bounds Green, where nineteen shelterers (mostly Belgian refugees) died on 13 October, and at Bank, where a huge bomb exploded on the evening of 11 January 1941, leaving a crater 36 m (120 ft) across. It blew open the sub-surface booking hall and killed fifty-six people on the platforms below. A long military Bailey bridge had to be erected to carry traffic over the demolished road junction outside the Bank and Royal Exchange.

Sloane Square on the District line is a cut-and-cover station almost on the surface. It had recently been refurbished with a new booking hall and escalators when it suffered a direct hit on 12 November 1940 at 10 p.m., just as a crowded train was about to depart. The station buildings and escalators were virtually destroyed and at least seventy-nine passengers were killed in the blast, with three more unaccounted for. An Underground motorman who survived a similar bomb attack on his train and helped his badly injured passengers later featured in a London Transport poster series, titled 'Seeing it Through', by official war artist Eric Kennington. Each of his six sitters was a staff member who had quietly and bravely 'carried on' during a dangerous Blitz incident.

Daily operation of the Underground continued throughout the war years, and with fewer incidents and interruptions than

**OPPOSITE:** 'Seeing it Through: Motorman': poster by Eric Kennington, 1944. Driver Frank Clarke kept his nerve driving his train through a Blitz raid, and was one of six London Transport staff depicted in morale-boosting posters by an official war artist.

**RIGHT:** The Bank station bombing on 12 January 1941 left fifty-six people dead when the Tube booking hall and escalators were blown open in a heavy raid. This was described simply as a 'bombed subway' in the press, with the Royal Exchange cropped out of the photograph.

had been predicted. Passenger numbers dropped considerably in 1940–41 during the heaviest period of the Blitz, when nearly 50,000 high-explosive bombs and millions of incendiaries fell on the city. The Underground, together with the buses, trams and trolleybuses, provided a vital daily service, which, in the words of *The Times*, 'kept London alive'.

Nearly 200 London Transport staff were killed while on duty, with a further 1,867 seriously injured in bombing incidents. There was severe damage to the LPTB's buildings, property and equipment, predictably worse on the roads than the railways. Some 19 railway cars, 166 buses and coaches, 69 trams and 15 trolleybuses were destroyed, some after a direct hit on a depot that damaged multiple vehicles. Incendiary bombs often set fire to a group of vehicles stored close together under cover, but dispersal on the streets or in open railway yards made them equally vulnerable.

Some sections of the system were put out of action for several months at a time, but services were never brought to a standstill. Where damage could not be repaired to allow reinstatement of rail services within a few days, a substitute bus service was introduced wherever possible. But in the stoic words of Michael Robbins, London Transport's official historian: 'The effect of air bombing was not so shattering as had been expected. In all, the damage done was severe but never crippling.'

Keeping London on the move was vital for the economy, for the war effort and above all for Londoners' morale. This achievement is all the more remarkable given that 22,500 experienced LPTB staff had been called up for military service at the outbreak of the war in 1939. As in the Great War, women were soon recruited to fill many of the jobs formerly carried out by men. The largest number were employed as bus conductors, but nearly 5,000 women worked on the Underground and in the engineering departments, often in physically demanding roles, particularly at Acton Railway Works and in the three power stations at Lots Road, Neasden and Greenwich.

The vital contribution of the women was singled out for praise at the time, as was the LPTB's commitment to providing suitable facilities for its new female intake, including nurseries for working mothers. Despite this, as transport historian David Bownes points out: 'Powerful trade union interests and resilient social prejudices ensured that women were usually paid less than their male colleagues and barred from certain skilled jobs such as driving.' Women had at last been granted a vote in elections, but their position in the workplace had not advanced dramatically since 1918 and was still regarded as temporary and 'for the duration' of the war. It would be another thirty years before there was a single female Tube driver in London.

LEFT: A female worker using a lathe at London Transport's Acton Works, 1941.

BELOW: Sloane Square station suffered a direct hit on 12 November 1940. It was 10 p.m., just as a crowded train was about to depart. The station buildings and escalators were virtually destroyed and at least seventy-nine passengers were killed in the blast.

OPPOSITE: This Underground car repaired after a Blitz attack by welding the undamaged sections of two separate cars together is now preserved at the Buckinghamshire Railway Centre at Quainton Road.

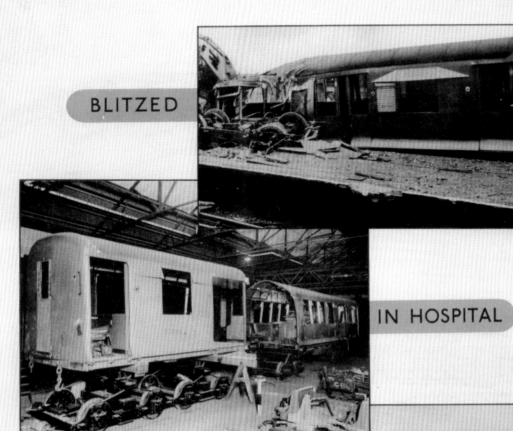

BLITZED

IN HOSPITAL

AT WORK AGAIN

Underground cars Nos. 013167 and 14233 were both "blitzed". One half of each car was beyond repair; the other two halves were repaired. London Transport's engineers "went to it" joined these–and a complete new car numbered 14233 is the result

Not all wartime loss of life on the Underground was due to enemy action. On 3 March 1943, there was an awful incident at Bethnal Green station, still under construction but handed over unfinished by London Transport to the local authority for wartime use as a public shelter. Some 173 people, many of them children, were crushed and suffocated to death on a stairwell after a mother carrying a baby tripped in the dark. The lack of a handrail, poor lighting and inadequate supervision by the police and ARP all apparently contributed to the disaster. A crowd may have hurried for the shelter on hearing the sound of new anti-aircraft rockets being tested in nearby Victoria Park, mistakenly believing there was an air raid in progress. A recently installed memorial sculpture near the station entrance now commemorates the victims of this terrible tragedy.

On government instructions, London Transport began to build eight new tunnels at a deeper level in 1940. These were to act as more secure shelters for public and military use. There were long-term plans to join some of them up and create a new express Tube paralleling the Northern line. In fact, the tunnels were used exclusively for military purposes from their completion in 1942 until the flying bomb attacks began in 1944, when five deep shelters on the Northern line axis – at Belsize Park, Camden Town, Stockwell, Clapham North and Clapham South – were belatedly opened up to

civilians. The Clapham South shelter can now be visited on a guided tour with the London Transport Museum's Hidden London programme.

These new tunnels were subdivided into two decks, and each shelter could theoretically hold up to 8,000 people, although they were never used to such an extent during the war. The express Tube idea, which would have been very expensive, was never developed after 1945. The Goodge Street deep shelter was reserved for military use during the war, mainly it seems by the US Army as a secure communications centre, although the secret activities carried out there are unknown. It was said to be intended as an operational headquarters for General Eisenhower, supreme commander of Allied forces, but there is no evidence that he ever used it or even visited during the run-up to the invasion of Europe in 1944. The name Eisenhower Centre was only adopted many years later in the 1980s, when the Goodge Street shelter was leased out and revamped to create an extensive, air-conditioned archive store for businesses.

The deep shelter at Clapham South found use as temporary accommodation after the war, notably housing for a few weeks a group of 200 Caribbean migrants, who arrived in Britain in 1948 on the MV *Empire Windrush*. The nearest labour exchange to Clapham South was on Coldharbour Lane in Brixton, so the men sought jobs and accommodation there.

**OPPOSITE, ABOVE:** The newly built, but unfinished tunnels for the Central line extension were the only Tube shelters available in the East End, but could be used all the time because the line was not yet open.

**LEFT AND OPPOSITE, BELOW:** Bethnal Green station opened in 1947 with the first part of the line to Stratford, complete with Modernist platform clocks with LT bullseyes for numerals and 1930s embossed tile designs by Harold Stabler. These features were restored or replicated in the 1990s.

**ABOVE:** Safe shelter though it was, Bethnal Green suffered one awful incident in 1943 that was not caused by enemy action. 173 people, many of them children, were crushed to death in a panic rush to one of the station stairways.

# Widening the War Effort

London Transport not only transported and sheltered both civilians and military personnel throughout the war, but it also made a significant contribution to the war effort through its workshops (while normal repair and servicing activities were reduced). Having gained experience servicing Spitfires and Hurricanes in the summer of 1940, the LPTB joined forces with four motor companies to form the London Aircraft Production Group, which built Handley Page Halifax heavy bombers for the Ministry of Aircraft Production. More than 700 aircraft were assembled over a four-year period at Acton and Chiswick in west London and at Aldenham and Leavesden in Hertfordshire. Some 80 per cent of the workforce had no previous engineering experience and more than half of them were women. London Transport staff also raised the cost of two new Spitfires themselves, which went into service with the RAF carrying the LPTB bullseye on the cockpit.

The Halifax assembly work at Aldenham took place in the newly built railway depot, which had been intended to house Tube cars for the Northern line extension from Edgware to Bushey Heath, a project abandoned after the war. Another almost completed part of the New Works Programme, the 3.2km (2 miles) of future Central line Tube tunnel between Leytonstone and Newbury Park, was converted by London Transport into a temporary aircraft electronic components facility for Plessey. The hidden underground factory opened in March 1942 and employed 2,000 workers on day and night shifts for the next three years until it was converted back to its original peacetime purpose after the war.

As the war reached its closing stages in the run-up to the invasion of Europe in 1944, Acton works became a centre for the overhaul of landing craft motors and the conversion of US Sherman tanks and Bren gun carriers, to enable them to drive through shallow water from landing craft on to the Normandy beaches on D-Day. Like the Halifax builders, most of the staff deployed on these projects were women with little or no engineering experience, but they all played their part in the successful delivery of equipment urgently needed in the final months of the war.

ABOVE, LEFT: One of the two Spitfires funded by LPTB staff, carrying the London Transport bullseye into action with the RAF.

LEFT: Handley Page Halifax bombers being assembled in what would have become a new Northern line depot at Aldenham. The Tube extension north of Edgware was cancelled after the war and the building became part of a new bus overhaul works.

ABOVE: The secret wartime underground factory making aircraft electronic equipment and components for Plessey housed in the new Central line tunnels near Redbridge, removed as soon as the war ended.

LEFT: The entrance to the deep shelter at Clapham South opened on the edge of Clapham Common in 1942.

BELOW, LEFT: Growing fresh micro greens and salad leaves in the former deep shelter at Clapham Common. This underground urban farm uses a hydroponic controlled environment.

BELOW, RIGHT: The circular entrance building to the Stockwell deep shelter is next to the war memorial and has been decorated with murals. These commemorate local heroes and heroines, including Violette Szabo. She lived nearby as a teenager and became an SOE agent during the Second World War before being captured and executed by the Nazis in 1945.

This led to Brixton becoming a focus for West Indian settlers from that point onwards, with successive arrivals making their way there and the growth of a local Caribbean community. In 1956, London Transport, suffering a post-war labour shortage, set up a direct recruitment drive in the Caribbean, which continued through the 1960s.

More recently, an innovative and enterprising new use for the Clapham North shelter has been found in the twenty-first century. It is now an urban farm, growing fresh micro greens and salad leaves using hydroponic systems and LED lighting technology. Crops are grown year-round in a controlled environment, unaffected by pests or the weather, and supplied directly to London restaurants and retailers. With no air miles and very short delivery distances, this fresh produce grown deep below the city has a minimal carbon footprint.

### The Return of Peace

With the end of the war in Europe in May 1945 and the election of a new Labour government, there was a clear expectation of change in Britain, but little clarity about what this might mean or how it could be achieved. London Transport issued a series of apologetic posters about the slow speed of rehabilitation and recovery from the damage and disruption caused by six years of enemy action. 'It takes TIME' was the placatory strapline on all of them.

With no money to improve facilities, London Transport could do little more than appeal to passengers to behave courteously towards each other and urge businesses to stagger working hours in the hope of relieving the peak hour crush. Neither approach had much impact, and both the usage of the system and rush hour overcrowding rose. The number of passengers using the LPTB's road and rail services reached a high point of 4,259 million in 1946, compared with 3,782 million in 1938–9. However, a resumption of the pre-war investment programme, overtaking the wartime arrears of maintenance and repair, and replacing worn-out rolling stock all looked unlikely.

Plans to resume the New Works Programme on the Underground were reviewed in the light of post-war financial difficulties. London Transport was authorized to proceed only with the unfinished eastern and western extensions of the Central line, which were completed to Epping and West Ruislip, respectively, between 1946 and 1949. Completion of the eastern extension branch through Redbridge and Gants Hill was considered a priority, with high passenger demand predicted along the Eastern Avenue suburban area in North Ilford, where the new Tube stations would be fed by bus routes.

On the other former London North Eastern Railway (LNER) branch, electrification to take the Tube north of Loughton to Epping was justified by the presence of new social housing

The dramatic 'Moscow' concourse at Gants Hill on the Central line eastern extension opened in 1947. This is a tribute to the design style of the Moscow Metro stations of 1935, which are double-ended with a central concourse opening out at full length on to the platforms. The benefits of spreading the crowds are less obvious at suburban Gants Hill, which is single-ended.

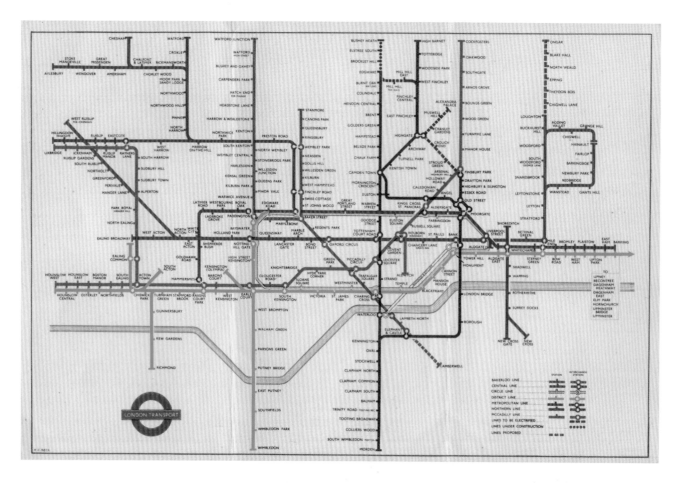

estates, notably a large new LCC estate at Debden with more than 4,000 flats and houses. The single-track country branch beyond Epping to Ongar remained a steam-worked shuttle service until 1957. This final electrification was hardly justifiable and a worthwhile traffic never developed. The Tube service to Ongar, still a shuttle with no through trains to London, which meant a change at Epping, was eventually closed down in 1994. The conductor rails were removed and the de-electrified line was sold by London Underground. After some difficult early years in private hands, the Epping–Ongar Railway now flourishes as a preserved steam railway.

Clearing the Plessey military components factory from the Redbridge tunnels in preparation for the Tube's arrival was a complex process. Getting the trains ready for the extended Central line services proved almost as difficult as finishing off the half-completed infrastructure. A new Tube depot at Hainault, ready in 1939 but then unused during the early war years, had been handed over to the US Army Transportation Corps in 1943 to assemble military rolling stock. This meant storing many complete Tube trains intended for the Central line extension out in the open at various sites for more than two years. Much of this stock had deteriorated quite badly by 1945 and nearly all of it required extra-heavy overhaul and complete rewiring before it could go back into public service.

The extension of the Central line in west London was more straightforward, and was all above ground alongside the Great Western Railway (GWR) main line from a junction at North Acton station. Much of the infrastructure work, including widening cuttings, embankments, bridges and some initial station rebuilding, had almost been completed by the time the New Works Programme was suspended in 1939–40. Most of this had been designed and carried out by the GWR rather than London Transport, unlike the eastern extension, where the only significant contribution of the main-line partner, the LNER, had been the rebuilding of Loughton station in 1939–40. The western extension was opened as far as Greenford in 1947 and on to West Ruislip two years later, although not through to Denham as originally planned.

All the new stations featured fluorescent lighting, which was first tried out at Piccadilly Circus in 1945 and installed throughout the Underground in the 1950s and 1960s. Strip lights were three times brighter than the old dim filament lamps, thus giving a harsh and efficient, if less cosy, illumination to trains, stations and escalators.

## The Austerity Years

With the application of Green Belt and other planning regulations after the war, there was little likelihood of substantial passenger traffic on the proposed Northern line

**OPPOSITE, ABOVE:** The 1948 Tube map, showing the almost completed eastern end of the Central line extension and the Northern line extensions to Alexandra Palace and Aldenham, soon to be abandoned.

**OPPOSITE, BELOW:** Hanger Lane station, on the western extension of the Central line to Greenford, opened with a temporary building in 1947. The permanent building completed in 1949 was a version of the pre-war design by Brian Lewis, with no tower and revised materials due to post-war steel shortages.

**ABOVE:** Tube trains reached Epping in 1949, but the steam shuttle to Ongar from here survived until 1957. This final section of the Central line to be electrified was closed by London Underground in 1994 and is now a preserved steam operation: the Epping & Ongar Railway.

**RIGHT:** A pre-war Standard stock motor car rewired and refurbished for the Central line extensions after wartime open storage. These trains were used until the early 1960s when some saw further operation with British Rail on the Isle of Wight.

Tube extension north of Edgware to Elstree and Bushey Heath. The plans were abandoned in 1950 and it was decided to make the unfinished Tube depot at Aldenham – used to build aircraft during the war – the basis of a large new bus overhaul works. London Transport's bus fleet had more than doubled in size since the 1920s, when Chiswick Works was opened by the London General Omnibus Company. By the 1950s, it was essential to provide more spacious and better equipped facilities for the overhaul of the massive standardized post-war bus fleet built up after 1947. Conversion and extension work to enable full-scale 'flowline' fleet overhaul to take place at Aldenham were completed in 1956.

By this time, all the remaining unfinished railway works of the 1935–40 programme had also been dropped. Electrification of the Northern line beyond Mill Hill East to Edgware was never carried out, and the tracks were eventually lifted. The old LNER branch line from Finsbury Park to Alexandra Palace via Crouch End and Highgate had been largely prepared for Tube services by late 1939, with new colour light signalling, electricity sub-stations and most of the necessary cabling installed. An increasingly unreliable LNER, then British Railways, steam service limped on until 1954, when the last passenger train ran.

Today, with the tracks removed, much of the route has been turned into a pleasant, leafy urban country walk.

Highgate surface station, rebuilt in 1939 by London Transport, is now an overgrown and crumbling ruin directly above the Tube station. The electricity sub-station for the Tube at Crouch End has become a youth club and Muswell Hill railway station has been demolished and replaced by a school. Abandoning this well-advanced project still looks like a shocking and substantial waste of resources, and it would now be far too costly to reinstate the line even as a light tramway. Sadly, Muswell Hill and Alexandra Palace will never be on the Tube system.

London Transport's inability to get government financial backing to complete these new railway projects in the immediate post-war period reflected both the economic austerity of these years and the new administrative framework created in 1947. The Labour Party's landslide victory in the general election of May 1945 was a prelude to the nationalization of many key British industries and public utilities over the next three years, many of which have been closed down or privatized since the 1980s.

On 1 January 1948, London Transport was nationalized along with the four main-line railway companies. Priority for capital investment was given to other essential areas of the economy, including house building, the new National Health Service and electricity generation. Within the public transport field, the needs of the badly run-down main-line railway

network took precedence. A British Transport Commission (BTC) was established to run the country's railways and canals as well as certain road services. The 'big four' private railway companies were all nationalized as 'British Railways' and the LPTB was replaced by a new London Transport Executive (LTE), also under the nationalized BTC umbrella but managed separately.

Ashfield had only recently retired, leaving his deputy, Lord Latham – the former leader of the LCC – to take over. Ashfield had been appointed as a founder member of the BTC but died in November 1948. He and Pick, who had died within months of leaving the LPTB seven years earlier and had never been replaced, were not succeeded by anyone with comparable drive and ability to take London Transport forward in the difficult years of post-war austerity.

Part of the problem for the LTE was that improvements to the Underground could never be justified on purely economic grounds. Cross-subsidy of the loss-making Tube by the buses, which had always made a profit, was no longer possible. Although passenger numbers on the buses reached record levels in the late 1940s, this was tempered by London Transport's need to concentrate on completing the tram replacement programme in 1950–52, which had been postponed while the Central line extensions were finished. They were still catching up rather than moving forward.

TOP AND ABOVE: London Transport built a large new station on the Central line at White City in 1947–50, designed with a second 'rush' ticket hall to cope with the large crowds visiting the stadium for greyhound racing and athletics. It won a Festival of Britain design award in 1951.

# 7 Towards a New Tube

PREVIOUS PAGES: Victoria has long been the busiest Underground station in London because of the huge transfer of commuters from the main-line station onto the Tube, but access has always been cramped and poor. At last a new entrance with lifts and escalators has been opened from Victoria Street in 2018 giving better access to both the District and Victoria lines.

OPPOSITE: 'Cut Travelling Time': Tom Eckersley's classic poster for the Victoria line when it opened in 1968, the first new Tube under central London for sixty years.

RIGHT: Using the automatic ticket machines at Piccadilly Circus, 1950. These hardy and reliable coin-operated machines, far more advanced than anything used on suburban services, were introduced on the Tube in 1937. They were used until the next generation of machines, the Underground Ticketing System (UTS), appeared in the 1980s.

## The New Elizabethan Age

After the Second World War, there was no shortage of ideas about how public transport could be improved in the London area. Members of the London Transport Executive (LTE) and the nationalized British Railways Board spent years working on the government's London Railway Plan to rationalize the capital's rail infrastructure and cut journey times. Their recommendations included the construction of several new Tube lines, a wildly optimistic pipe dream given the government's financial position. The brave new world of a rationally planned and rebuilt city failed to emerge in post-war London and there was no overall transport strategy to underpin the city's recovery.

A pattern emerged that has blighted most attempts to solve road and rail transport problems in London since the 1940s and continues in the twenty-first century. It is the familiar progression from setting up a government committee, to delivering a report followed by limited public debate, to eventual action about half a generation or fifteen years later. In the course of time, a single new scheme may become less relevant or overshadowed by other ideas. As time passes, political priorities and financial circumstances change, and big infrastructure projects are delayed, only taking place at extended intervals. Every delay and cost increase leads to greater public disillusion in the 'experts' who plan a scheme

and the politicians who may eventually approve it but fail to see it through. Sometimes nobody seems to win. This applies to both road and rail schemes, but a particularly depressing pattern of slow development on the Underground's big projects stands out. New Tube lines for London have followed a regular ten- to twenty-year cycle from the late 1940s up to the present day.

A new Tube railway (known originally as Route C) running right under the centre of the city, linking key main-line termini and running out to the north-east, was prioritized from the various recommendations made in a report of 1949, but not acted upon. It was finally opened twenty years later, in 1969, as the Victoria line. The limited first stage of the next new Tube opened ten years later again, in 1979 (the Jubilee line), but the main section of this line was not completed until the eve of the millennium in 1999. Finally, a main-line-sized Tube was built under the city from 2010 (Crossrail, later renamed the Elizabeth line), scheduled to open in 2018 but delayed for another year. This pattern was not predictable or linked to any economic cycles in the city's history, but it certainly underlines the tediously slow process of agreeing, funding and implementing large public infrastructure projects that became characteristic of modern Britain after the Second World War.

At the start of the 1950s, opinion about the experience of Underground travel was divided. The London evening papers were full of reports of overcrowding, delays and minor mishaps apparently caused by out-of-date equipment, but this was familiar stuff and it has continued ever since. For others, particularly visitors to London, the post-war Underground retained much of its pre-war reputation for cleanliness, efficiency and reliability, despite the under-investment. Take journalist and broadcaster Maurice Gorham, who claimed in his book *Londoners*, published in 1951:

> The Tubes remain the most efficient transport system in the world. Anyone who has experienced the Paris Metro and the New York Subway will agree that the Tube is the most comfortable for the habitual traveller and much the easiest for the stranger who is trying to find his way.

The international comparison with Paris and New York is revealing, reflecting a renewed confidence in London's place in the world and a feeling that the country as a whole was getting back on its feet again. Gorham's book was no doubt aimed at New Yorkers who might be attracted to London as tourists, rather than Londoners who were far less likely to be making the expensive trip to either New York or Paris. Nevertheless, there was a clear optimism seen both at the Festival of Britain in 1951, promoted under the strapline 'a tonic for the nation', and at the Queen's coronation two years later, which was said to herald a 'new Elizabethan age'.

Against this background, there were high hopes for a second 'golden age' of public transport in the city. London Transport effectively became the city's first tourist agency, promoting transport information alongside London's heritage and visitor attractions, all easily reached by bus, coach or train. But behind this engaging façade, the Underground was about to enter a decade of chronic under-investment, which was to cause long-term damage to the transport system.

John Elliot, who succeeded Lord Latham as chairman of the LTE in 1953 and was knighted the following year, had a long and successful career in railway management, which began with his role as the Southern Railway's (SR) first public relations officer in the 1920s. He was a great admirer of Lord Ashfield and Frank Pick, who had both assisted him in his early days at the SR, but thirty years on Elliot found there was little scope for using the successful approach honed by the LPTB's dynamic duo.

Circumstances had completely changed, and London's transport improvement requirements after the war were still seen by government as unaffordable extras, ranked well behind the needs of British Railways for the national network. Investment in London Transport continued to fall in the early 1950s, with capital spending on the Underground declining from £877,000 in 1950 to around £300,000 in each of the years 1952 to 1954. This was a pitifully small sum that barely covered the basic maintenance of assets valued at £93 million.

**LEFT:** Plans were prepared in 1937 to build a new integrated bus and Tube station at Newbury Park for when the extended Central line arrived. This was delayed by the war and financial cutbacks afterwards, which meant only Oliver Hill's Modernist concrete bus stand was built, while the old 1903 railway station remained alongside when the line was electrified in 1947.

**OPPOSITE:** A platform scene on the Bakerloo line at Piccadilly Circus in the late 1950s. The only thing that has changed here since the 1930s is the lighting: this was the first Tube station to be fitted with fluorescent strip lighting throughout at the end of the war.

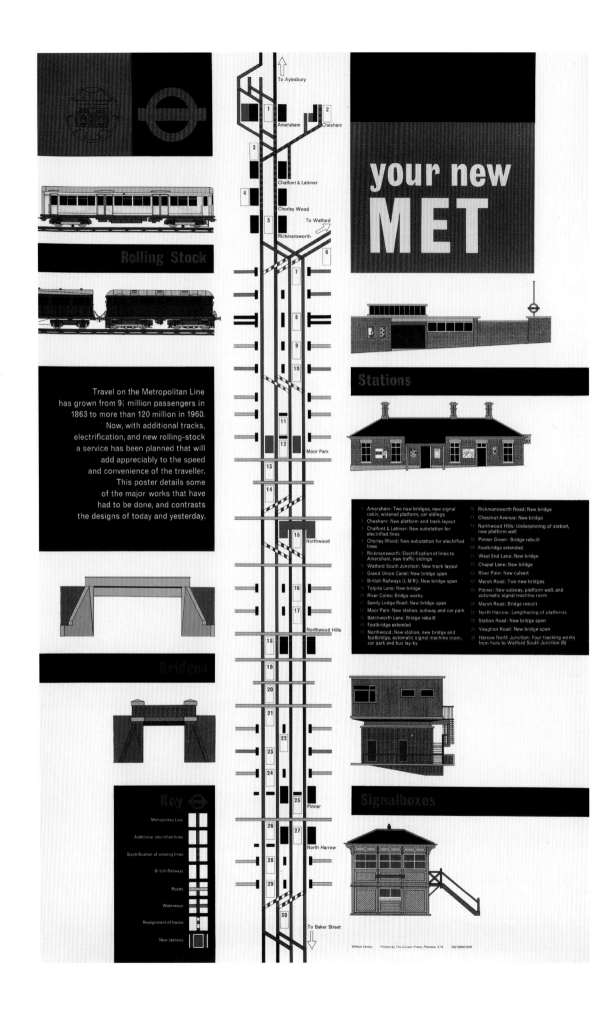

Rolling Stock

Travel on the Metropolitan Line
has grown from 9½ million passengers in
1863 to more than 120 million in 1960.
Now, with additional tracks,
electrification, and new rolling-stock
a service has been planned that will
add appreciably to the speed
and convenience of the traveller.
This poster details some
of the major works that have
had to be done, and contrasts
the designs of today and yesterday.

Bridges

Key

Metropolitan Line

Additional electrified lines

Electrification of existing lines

British Railways

Roads

Waterways

Realignment of tracks

New stations

your new
MET

Stations

1 Amersham: Two new bridges, new signal cabin, widened platform, car sidings
2 Chesham: New platform and track layout
3 Chalfont & Latimer: New substation for electrified lines
4 Chorley Wood: New substation for electrified lines
5 Rickmansworth: Electrification of lines to Amersford, new traffic sidings
6 Watford South Junction: New track layout
7 Grand Union Canal: New bridge span
8 British Railways (L M R): New bridge span
9 Tolpits Lane: New bridge
10 River Colne: Bridge works
11 Sandy Lodge Road: New bridge span
12 Moor Park: New station, subway and car park
13 Batchworth Lane: Bridge rebuilt
14 Footbridge extended
15 Northwood: New station, new bridge and footbridge, automatic signal machine room, car park and bus lay-by

16 Rickmansworth Road: New bridge
17 Chestnut Avenue: New bridge
18 Northwood Hills: Underpinning of station, new platform wall
19 Pinner Green: Bridge rebuilt
20 Footbridge extended
21 West End Lane: New bridge
22 Chapel Lane: New bridge
23 River Pinn: New culvert
24 Marsh Road: Two new bridges
25 Pinner: New subway, platform wall, and automatic signal machine room
26 Marsh Road: Bridge rebuilt
27 North Harrow: Lengthening of platforms
28 Station Road: New bridge span
29 Vaughan Road: New bridge span
30 Harrow North Junction: Four tracking works from here to Watford South Junction (6)

Signalboxes

William Fenton    Printed by The Curwen Press, Plaistow, E.13.    758/100SM 0065

Lack of investment inevitably led to piecemeal service upgrades and smaller one-off capital projects, such as the electrification of the little-used Epping to Ongar branch in 1957, which finally completed the Central line extension scheme, and the construction of a new £1-million depot for the District line at Upminster in 1959. The modernization and refurbishment of the outer Metropolitan line, another hangover from the 1930s, were finally authorized in 1956 and completed in phases between 1960 and 1962. This £3.5-million scheme was primarily designed to relieve congestion at Harrow-on-the-Hill and to extend electrification from Rickmansworth to Amersham and Chesham, which were still served by ex-Metropolitan Railway steam-hauled trains. This time, funding proved easier to secure because the proposals were broadly in tune with government policy to stimulate the expansion of commuter towns beyond the Green Belt by developing existing services.

The laying of additional tracks north of Harrow also improved the frequency of main-line railway services into Marylebone, which shared part of the route with London Transport over the former Metropolitan & Great Central Joint line, still used by Chiltern Railways today. The non-electrified section of the Metropolitan line beyond Amersham to Aylesbury was transferred to British Railways in 1961. This made the newly electrified Amersham station the furthest point from central London on the Underground, and finally ended the use of steam locomotives on London Transport passenger services.

Rather surprisingly, a small fleet of steam engines survived, pulling Underground engineers' trains for another ten years and outlasting all steam operation on British Railways. The end of steam and electric locomotive haulage on the Metropolitan in 1961 also meant the end of antiquated wooden-bodied compartment carriages on the Underground, some of which dated back to the late 1890s. They were replaced with new open saloon aluminium-bodied A60 stock trains. These operated on all outer Metropolitan line services until the next generation of surface stock trains was introduced in 2010–12.

### The Victoria Line

All this time, Elliot and his team had been working hard, although unsuccessfully, to secure government funding for more ambitious projects. Chief among these was the proposed deep-level Tube line from Victoria to Walthamstow, estimated to cost in the region of £50 million. Elliot recognized the public relations limitations of referring to this project as Route C and renamed it the Victoria line in 1955. London Transport began a concerted strategy of lobbying, using every opportunity to make the case for the line and diverging from the traditional pre-war arguments for new lines. This proposal marked an

**ABOVE:** The final days of steam operation at Rickmansworth on the Metropolitan line, 1961. The steam engine on the right has just come off the southbound train from Aylesbury, which will be taken on to Baker Street by electric loco No. 7. The loco change took just three minutes.

**OPPOSITE:** A teaser poster by William Fenton issued in 1960, highlighting some of the improvements that Metropolitan line passengers could expect over the next couple of years. Wisely, there is no boasting about completion dates or costs.

**ABOVE, RIGHT:** New silver A stock trains at Wembley Park, introduced in 1961.

**ABOVE, FAR RIGHT:** A guard on an A stock train, 1962. One-person operation was introduced on the Metropolitan line in 1986. The trains were modified but not replaced until 2015.

**RIGHT:** The interior of an A stock Metropolitan line train, 1961. The red, green and black seating fabric was a new design used extensively.

# Silver Trains

London Transport's experience with aircraft construction when it built Halifax bombers during the Second World War had an unexpected benefit with regard to the design of new buses and trains in the 1950s. The first generation of post-war Underground trains followed the smooth semi-streamlined body shape devised in the 1930s for deep-level Tube trains (1938 stock) and the flare-sided appearance of the larger sub-surface stock (O, P and Q38 stock). When the District line needed new trains based on the same template, the war supplies of steel were very limited, so designers turned to a metal that had been widely used in aircraft construction. Aluminium alloys had been used before in tram and bus body panels but never for the structure of a whole vehicle. Lightweight aluminium was easily available and, although it was more expensive than steel at that time, engineers calculated that the 16 per cent saving in weight would lead to power savings. Aluminium is also rustproof and therefore lasts longer than steel.

A car of R49 stock was displayed at the Festival of Britain in 1951, with one end left unpainted to highlight the new aluminium material. Although the exhibition car was subsequently resprayed in London Transport red before entering service, successful weathering trials on unpainted aluminium panels led to the introduction of an experimental eight-car 'silver' train in 1952. A year later, the decision was taken to leave all new trains unpainted and thus save the cost of regular repainting. The new silver trains were striking, modern and good for publicity, although within a few months their silver sparkle dulled down to a matt grey finish. A similar experiment a few years later with an unpainted aluminium Routemaster bus was not well received by the public, and for the time being London Transport's buses retain their red painted livery.

The minimalist look continued on the Underground with the 1959 and 1962 Tube stock, the Metropolitan line A stock and all subsequent new trains through the 1970s and 1980s. It was only with the appearance of train graffiti tags in the late 1980s, which damaged unpainted train bodies and were difficult to remove, that it was decided to revert to painting all London Underground trains in a standard corporate red, blue and white colour scheme.

**ABOVE, LEFT:** The first silver Tube stock enters service in mint condition, 1957.

**ABOVE, RIGHT:** Removing graffiti from an unpainted aluminium train at Neasden depot, 1995.

**RIGHT:** Current Victoria line stock, introduced fully painted in London Underground red, white and blue livery, 2009.

ABOVE: Afternoon traffic jam at Elephant & Castle, 1966, with no bus priority lanes provided.

RIGHT: Trying to encourage people out of their cars, 1965. The posters were popular but bus use continued to decline for the next thirty years.

important change in underground railway planning. Instead of further suburban extensions from the existing central area network, which had been the pattern since the Bakerloo passed Paddington in 1915, a new Tube crossing the central area and connecting with all existing lines was proposed.

The Victoria line was intended to provide quicker internal service across central London and to relieve congestion on other lines, particularly the Piccadilly and the Charing Cross branch of the Northern. The route and interchanges with existing lines would help to distribute the increasing numbers of outer suburban passengers commuting through the British Rail terminals at Victoria, Euston, St Pancras and King's Cross. The centre had been left in the pattern of 1907 for too long; the outward move of residential settlement had created, perhaps paradoxically, a need for better rail facilities within the inner ring. This chimed with the post-war encouragement by government of development in the New Towns created beyond London's Green Belt and the growth of longer-distance commuting from outside the existing suburban ring.

London Transport began a campaign to persuade politicians and the public that, although the line could not be self-supporting because so much of its large traffic would be diverted from existing, albeit overcrowded, means of transport, its benefits to London made it essential that the construction costs were met somehow. The scheme

was put before the Chambers committee of inquiry, which reported in 1955 in favour of going ahead and not abandoning or postponing the scheme 'because on the basis of direct revenue or direct expenditure it appears to be unprofitable'. The committee thought that expenditure on underground railways was preferable to expenditure on roads, a conclusion supported in 1956 by the influential study group Political and Economic Planning. These were encouraging noises, but government approval was still some way off.

Each year, London Transport continued to promote the advantages of the new line, in reports to the public through the press, radio and television and internally in memoranda via the British Transport Commission (BTC) to the minister. But the government remained in thrall to private road transport, opening the first section of the M1 motorway in 1959 and encouraging various traffic management schemes in London in a vain effort to stem the growing tide of congestion from private cars. One-way streets, flyovers, underpasses and parking meters had all been introduced by the 1950s, but they made little impact other than shifting the jams from one pinch point to the next. Sitting in a traffic queue in one's own private car was evidently preferable to being stuck on a bus. At a Conservative Party meeting in 1957, prime minister Harold Macmillan made his famous comment about the British people having 'never had it so good'. Rising wages

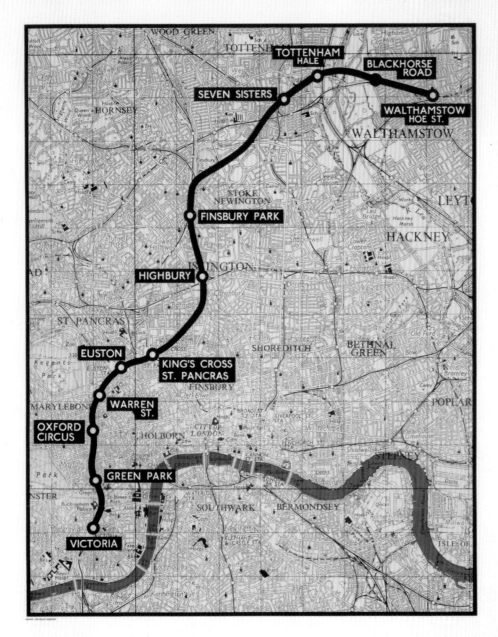

# VICTORIA LINE

# NOW UNDER CONSTRUCTION

- Oxford Circus to Victoria in 4 minutes.
- Welded rails and sound-proofing for smooth, quiet travel.
- Eleven stations with interchange to and from other lines.
- Direct link between Victoria, Oxford Circus, King's Cross and Euston.

- Euston to Green Park in 6 minutes.
- New ventilation techniques giving fresh air without draughts.
- Up to 32,000 passengers an hour in either direction.
- New trains with every device for speed and comfort.

LEFT: Victoria line poster, 1965, before the Brixton extension was agreed.

OPPOSITE: Brixton station opened with a bland single-storey street entrance in 1971, replaced with this dramatic giant roundel in the early 2000s.

and low unemployment were enabling more people to buy their own cars and abandon public transport for good.

Between 1950 and 1965, the number of private cars licensed in the London Transport area quadrupled, rising from 480,000 to 1,920,000. As more people had access to personal transport, they used public transport less, particularly for leisure travel. Meanwhile, television sets appeared in a growing number of homes, particularly after the introduction of a commercial channel in 1955. This cheap home entertainment meant Londoners took fewer trips out to the cinema, theatre and football matches, further reducing leisure travel on evenings and at weekends.

The number of passengers carried by London Transport's road services fell by nearly 40 per cent between 1948 and 1962, a drop encouraged by a seven-week bus strike in 1958. Passengers lost confidence in the increasingly unreliable service, and the traditional cross-subsidy of the Underground by profitable bus services was no longer possible by the late 1950s. To London Transport's evident surprise, passenger figures on the Underground held up quite well throughout the 1950s, with the 703 million journeys made in 1949 only falling to 668 million by 1962. The average Tube commute was longer than most bus journeys and there were fewer satisfactory alternatives. But as a sub-division of the BTC, which had the much larger responsibility for the whole of British Railways and

no direct access to the Ministry of Transport, the LTE – and the Underground in particular – was not seen as a priority for government spending.

London Transport's campaign to get the Victoria line under way moved on from persuasion to a full-scale practical trial in 1960, when authority was given for work costing £1 million to commence on a mile of experimental twin tunnels. This was to test newly developed methods of tunnel lining in concrete and cast iron. The trial was carried out on a section of the planned route between Finsbury Park and Seven Sisters and the method was to be incorporated in the future railway when it was constructed. Meanwhile, the trial was of course an astutely placed foot in the door that was widely publicized as if it were the first stage of the Victoria line getting under way. The LTE's annual report in 1961 duly described its success and announced that an early start could be made as soon as authority was received. With carefully chosen words, the LTE now claimed that the line *must* be constructed if the LTE were 'to fulfil their statutory duty to provide adequate services in the London area'.

In 1960, a cost/benefit analysis had been published that claimed a net social benefit for the first part of the M1 motorway. Early in 1962, London Transport followed up with a similar study on the Victoria line carried out by two Oxford University academics and independent economists. Their

The original 1967 Victoria line trains were completely redesigned internally in the 1990s with new lighting and seating before the entire fleet was replaced in 2007. This is the car used by the Queen at the opening in 1969 (see page 224) after refurbishment. It is now preserved in the London Transport Museum's collection.

report argued that although the railway would clearly not cover its operating costs, there would be a substantial 'social' rate of return. This was the first time that a case had been made for a new Tube that was not justified on financial grounds alone, and it seems to have been the final persuader for the government.

For some months, discussions had been under way about abolishing the BTC and making both London Transport and British Railways directly, but separately, responsible to the Ministry of Transport. In August 1962, the LTE was at last given the go-ahead to proceed with the construction of the Victoria line and it was announced that under the Transport Act of 1962 a new London Transport Board (the LTB) would take over its management from 1 January 1963. Just as the centenary of the world's first underground railway was being celebrated, London could look forward to the arrival of the first new Tube railway to be built below the city in fifty years.

By the end of 1963, contracts had been placed for more than £22 million worth of work, including all the shields and tunnel lining. More than twenty working shafts had been sunk and over thirty working sites occupied. As the entire line was built deep below the surface, little could be seen from above. The most visible sign of activity for Londoners was the construction of a massive steel platform over the road junction at Oxford Circus in 1963. This was the largest and most complex station reconstruction site on the line and

its temporary new roof was soon known as the 'umbrella'. The steel cover allowed building work to take place on a new station ticket hall immediately below it, while traffic continued to flow along Oxford Street above without interruption. The umbrella remained in place for five years until just before the first section of the Victoria line opened in 1968.

The physical construction of the Victoria line was extremely intricate owing to the warren of existing tunnels and passages through which it had to thread its way. It took just over six years to complete, including a world record for soft ground tunnelling of 140 m (470 ft) in one week. The build programme had been carefully planned using a computer-aided system of network analysis, which at the time was quite advanced and sophisticated, but slippages crept in for various reasons that could not have been predicted. Major factors were the time taken to assemble the necessary expertise at the start and the constant shortage of manpower, especially miners. From 1962 onwards, there was a construction boom for new commercial offices in central London, which made competition in the building industry fierce.

As complications and delays mounted, it was decided to have a phased opening of the new line, beginning with the outer Walthamstow to Highbury & Islington section on 1 September 1968, then on to Warren Street from 1 December. These sections were both opened without ceremony and the

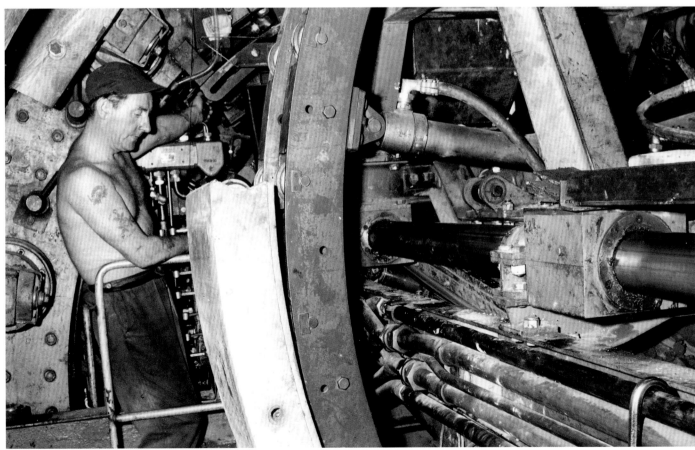

LEFT: The Queen talking to Eric Wilkins, LT's chief public relations officer, at the royal opening of the Victoria line in 1969.

BELOW: New technology in action, 1970. The Victoria line control centre at Cobourg Street, near Euston, where the train regulator and line controller supervise operation of the line remotely.

OPPOSITE, LEFT: Victoria line train operator, 1969. The train is computer-controlled but the driver operates the doors and can take over in an emergency.

OPPOSITE, RIGHT: Victoria line poster, 1969.

formal inauguration of the whole line through to Victoria was carried out by Queen Elizabeth II at Green Park station on 7 March 1969.

There was a brief hold-up on the Queen's arrival when the new automatic ticket machine rejected her equerry's sixpences and London Transport's chief public relations officer had to rush forward with a replacement shilling. After that slightly embarrassing hiccup, the Tube's new technology performed perfectly as the Queen used her yellow magnetic strip ticket to open the barrier and rode a gleaming silver escalator down to the platform. Here, in her opening speech, she noted the pioneering role of Britain in building underground railways, praised the 'arduous work of the miners whose efforts made this project possible' and recalled the role of her great-grandfather, Edward VI, who when still Prince of Wales had opened the first electric Tube in 1890 and the Central London Railway in 1900. She herself had a 'vivid memory' of her only previous Tube trip as a young princess, long before she became queen. She and her sister, Princess Margaret, had been taken on an educational visit in 1939 and were photographed by the press entering Tottenham Court Road station.

Thirty years later, the Queen took her place in the cab of a new train alongside driver Francis Fountain of Tottenham, who showed her how to 'drive' it on a short run to Oxford Circus.

Operation of Victoria line trains was in fact fully automated by a computer-controlled system developed by London Transport engineers in the early 1960s and now applied to passenger service for the first time. With the introduction of automatic train operation, the driver had only to press the two buttons on the cab dashboard to start the train. His principal role was to operate the train doors and to override the automated system in case of emergency. Automatic signals and coded electronic impulses in the track were coordinated from a central control room at the top of a new office block near Euston. Fully automatic operation at a distance with no controller on board was perfectly feasible, but London Transport did not believe the public would accept unmanned trains at this time, when all other Underground trains had both a driver and a guard.

London Transport's publicity machine went into overdrive for the Victoria line launch. There were posters, leaflets, a commemorative book, a special General Post Office postmark, a series of documentary films describing every aspect of the construction and even the novelty (for the Underground) of a television commercial. The television advertisement was one of the first to feature a technique that later became commonplace, with a slot at the start and end of commercial breaks emphasizing the short time it now took to get from Victoria to Oxford Circus on the new line.

ABOVE LEFT AND RIGHT: Two views of the Victoria line showing the silver, grey and light blue colour palette that was applied to trains, tiles and ticket machines. Design consultants Misha Black and the DRU gave everything the smart but cold look of aluminium and stainless steel.

LEFT : Railman Lloyd Manning and ticket collector Lucille Richmond with the 'ton of bricks' tiling at Brixton, 1971. This was the first Tube extension south of the river since the 1920s.

OPPOSITE: The tile motifs on the Victoria line platforms were the only splash of colour at the twelve original stations on the line in 1969.

Public service on the Victoria line began at 3 p.m. on the opening day. London Transport press notices claimed that it would be 'the most highly automated and technically advanced underground railway in the world and in the peak hours its trains will be able to carry 25,000 passengers an hour in each direction – the equivalent of eleven motorway lanes'. This proud boast was based on the new automatically controlled trains providing a 20 per cent faster service than other lines and the additional efficiency of automatic ticket machines and gates, together with a closed-circuit television system to monitor passenger flows and loudspeakers to make service announcements.

Despite intensive testing, innovative equipment took time to bed down under the pressure of daily use by London's commuters. On the first day of operation, a power failure put the twelve automatic ticket machines at Victoria, the busiest transfer station from a main line terminus, out of action in the rush hour. A queue of passengers stretched from the Underground booking office to the British Railways platforms. The expression 'a dodgy solenoid' soon became an in-joke for booking clerks faced with unexplained technological mishaps.

The new line was not greeted publicly with quite the triumphal quality of the Underground's own publicity. Economist and journalist Anthony Sampson, writing in the *Observer*, described it as 'extraordinarily bleak', its 'late lavatorial style, with shiny grey tiles, harsh strip lighting . . . the long echoing passages with bare black ribs, seeming to be leading to some mass underground grave'. He went on to praise the Paris Métro's new Louvre station, decorated with replicas of museum objects, which he contrasted with the 'public squalor' of the Tube. 'Surely the Victoria line needs something more than automatic tickets and coloured tiles if it is really to be (as its advertisements proclaim) London's pride.'

For all its impressive technology, the appearance of the Victoria line was not welcoming, and it was certainly a contrast to the warm but functional pre-war designs of the Pick and Holden era. It was designed in-house by London Transport's chief architect Kenneth Seymour, with design consultancy advice from Misha Black and the Design Research Unit, but somehow the potentially creative partnership of architects, designers and engineers was lost. Black defended the clinical grey look of the stations, with silver trains and escalators, arguing that 'the stations may be criticized for appearing visually unexciting, but we consider that preferable to a transient popularity without lasting qualities'.

Fifty years on, it is difficult to see what Black thought those 'lasting qualities' were on the Victoria line. The only decorative features to liven up the grey platforms were the tile designs by artists, on the walls above the seat recesses, which were combined together in a rather leaden poster design that was

# TILE MOTIFS ON THE VICTORIA LINE

*by Julia Black*
An adaptation of a William Morris design. He was born and worked for a time in Walthamstow where a museum displays examples of his work.

*by Hans Unger*
The black horse also appears as a sculpture, by David McFall, on the exterior of the station.

*by Edward Bawden*
The name is derived from a ferry over the river Lea in earlier times. The word 'hale' is said to be a corruption of 'haul'; or perhaps 'hail'.

*by Hans Unger*
The seven sisters were seven trees which gave a name to the locality.

*by Tom Eckersley*
The crossed pistols refer to the duelling that took place here when this was outside the edge of London.

*by Edward Bawden*
The high bury, manor or castle, was destroyed at the time of the Peasants' Revolt (1381).

*by Tom Eckersley*
A literal design based on a cross and crowns. The King concerned (if there ever was one) is not identified.

*by Tom Eckersley*
A reminder of the Doric Arch which stood on the station site.

*by Crosby/Fletcher/Forbes*
A maze or Warren as a pun on the name. A solution is possible for the traveller with time to spare.

*by Hans Unger*
A device to incorporate the circle of the circus with the linking of the Bakerloo, Central and Victoria Lines.

*by Hans Unger*
A bird's eye view of the trees in the park against the green background of the grass.

*by Edward Bawden*
The great Queen herself, from a silhouette by Benjamin Pearce. A plaque in the ticket hall records the visit of Queen Elizabeth to open the Victoria Line in March 1969.

All these motif designs, specially commissioned for the twelve stations so far open on the Victoria Line, are reproduced in full colour in a folder obtainable price 1/- at any main London Transport Travel Enquiry Office (including those on the Victoria Line at Euston, Oxford Circus and Victoria Stations). Or post free from the Public Relations Officer, 55 Broadway, S.W.1. Copies of this poster cost 12/6.

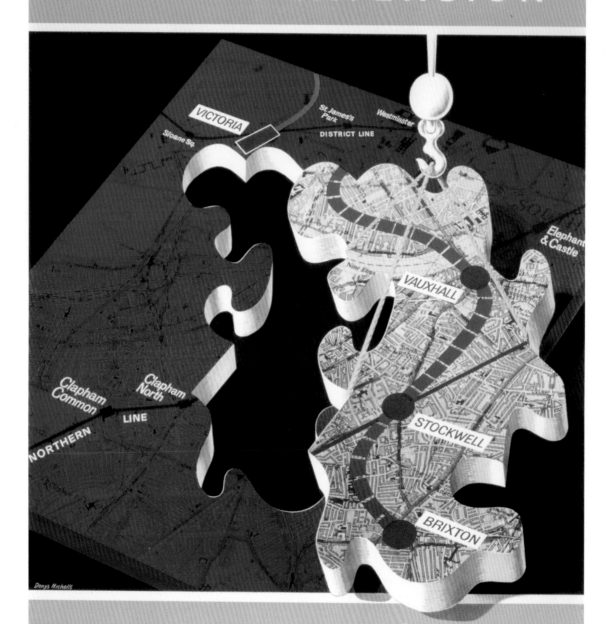

# VICTORIA LINE
## BRIXTON EXTENSION

**completing the picture**

available from travel enquiry offices. Only one of the stations, Blackhorse Road, has a surface building, which is in a dull and bland 1960s style. Severe budget restrictions meant that infrastructure standards were lower than those on older lines, with narrower platforms, concrete steps instead of a third escalator, unfinished ceilings and domestic-bathroom-quality tiling that soon began to drop off the walls.

The Victoria line was a remarkable achievement, which stretched the available technology and resources to the limit. Not everything worked: the automatic ticketing system failed and the gates were removed in 1972. The benefits of automation would only be realized when a more robust system was installed across the whole network in the 1980s.

With its pioneering automated computer control system, the new Victoria line was to be the last outright world-leadership achievement for the London Underground. The Bay Area Rapid Transit system in San Francisco opened in September 1972, featuring both automatic train control and ticketing. Three years on, there had been no further significant developments in London, although the planned extension of the Victoria line south of the river to Brixton had been achieved and opened in 1971.

This was a modest extension of only 5.6 km (3.5 miles), but it had to be built through difficult waterlogged and gravelly ground at the intermediate station sites planned on both sides

of the Thames. At Vauxhall, a cofferdam was required to keep river water out of the ticket hall just below street level. The deeper ground through which the escalator shaft was to be sunk had to be frozen solid using a refrigerated liquid passed through a network of pipes before excavation could begin. This was another novel technique for the Victoria line, first used at Tottenham Hale and required again at Pimlico, the final station to be built.

Pimlico, which opened in 1972, did not meet the usual interchange requirements for Victoria line stations, but it was a useful site for the local residential community and immediately provided better access to the Tate Gallery (now Tate Britain) on its Embankment site, then only served directly by bus. As predicted, the Victoria line was not a great revenue earner for London Transport, but it soon proved incredibly popular. By the early twenty-first century, it had become the fourth busiest line in terms of passenger numbers and the most intensively used, carrying in excess of 13,000 passengers per mile. This was four times the original forecast.

OPPOSITE: Poster for the Brixton extension of the Victoria line, 1967. This was started before the initial line was opened to ensure continuity in the construction teams. The final station, Pimlico, was not approved until 1968 and opened in 1972.

ABOVE, LEFT AND RIGHT: Main escalators at Victoria, 1969, and additional escalators from the new station entrance, 2019.

RIGHT: Automatic entrance and exit barriers on the Victoria line, 1971.

# 8 Renewal

## The Politics of Transport

The 1970s was a difficult decade for public transport in London and it saw the start of serious political feuding between local and national politicians, which continued until the end of the century. A new local authority, the Greater London Council (GLC), was created in 1965, covering an area twice the size of the old London County Council, which it replaced. From 1 January 1970, the government transferred financial and broad policy control of London Transport to the GLC. It was a logical move that put London's public transport under the authority responsible for broader strategic planning in the metropolis. It also enabled the GLC to start with a clean sheet by wiping out all capital debts incurred during the construction of the Victoria line. However, control of major future capital funding still rested with central government, which weakened the GLC's ability to make any significant changes from the start.

London Transport's troubled fourteen years of control began promisingly for the Underground. In 1971, the second year of GLC control, two important new capital projects got under way: the extension of the Piccadilly line to Heathrow began in April, and five months later work started on the new Fleet line, later to morph into the Jubilee line.

Heathrow, which was designated as London's principal airport just after the war, had become the busiest in the world by the late 1960s, dealing with 14 million passengers a year and expanding rapidly. But its transport links with central London were poor. London Transport and British Rail (BR) each prepared their own scheme for a rail link: one an extension of the Piccadilly line from Hounslow West and the other a new BR branch off the Southern Region line at Feltham, which would provide a fast service to Victoria.

Late in 1969, just before the GLC took over London Transport, the government set up a Heathrow Link Steering Group to study the options. Following the now familiar approach of a cost/benefit analysis, as used on the Victoria line, the Piccadilly line extension emerged as the group's favoured option. This was principally because the Tube could offer airline passengers a direct journey to various destinations in central London rather than depositing them at Victoria. In addition, the Tube service would offer a much greater frequency than BR could provide.

The £25-million project was approved by the GLC in 1970 in the expectation of the same 25/75 per cent division of cost between it and central government that had been agreed for the Brixton extension of the Victoria line. In a foretaste of financial wrangles to come, the physical work on the Heathrow extension actually began before a final settlement of the cost share had been reached.

The Piccadilly line extension was built mainly using the cut-and-cover method, from the rebuilt Hounslow West station as far as Hatton Cross, on the edge of the airport, and it opened in 1975. The extension was then projected along 2 km (1¼ miles) of twin Tube tunnels under the runways to Heathrow Central. The Queen made her second visit to the Tube as monarch to formally open the final section on 16 December 1977, at which point London could proudly claim to have the world's first direct rail link between a principal airport and the centre of a capital city. In its first full year of operation, the Heathrow extension was used by 8 million passengers.

This was not the end of the Heathrow story of course, as the airport's continued expansion led to the creation of a loop extension to serve the new Terminal 4 in 1986 and a branch to Terminal 5 in 2008. Another rail route to London was also opened in 1998, branded the Heathrow Express. It ran into Paddington rather than Victoria, which had been the original BR proposal. By this time, BR had been privatized, and the new service was developed by the British Airports Authority in partnership with what became Network Rail. Heathrow Express offers a more expensive, though much faster, non-stop rail link with central London at Paddington. Piccadilly line trains stop at more than fifteen stations and take over an hour to reach central London from Heathrow, but they do run through the whole West End area rather than terminating at the western edge.

## From Fleet to Jubilee

The other new Tube construction project started in 1971 had its origins, like the Victoria line, in the London Plan Working Party Report of 1949. It remained no more than an outline suggestion until the late 1960s, when detailed proposals were drawn up for what was then called the Fleet line. The plan involved the new line taking over the Stanmore branch of the Bakerloo line as far as Baker Street, then running in new tunnels via Bond Street and Green Park to Charing Cross. The main benefit of this would be to relieve the most heavily used section of the Underground network: the Bakerloo line between Baker Street and Oxford Circus.

A second stage of the project would take the line east of Charing Cross under Fleet Street (hence the original name) and through the City to Fenchurch Street. A third stage would involve running under the river via Surrey Docks and New Cross to Lewisham and possibly on to Thamesmead, which were all neglected parts of south-east London that had never been served by the Tube.

But in the 1970s, the prospect of these later stages of the new line being achieved rapidly slipped away. London Transport and the GLC became bogged down in acrimonious disputes about the day-to-day management of resources and revenue funding. Both Labour and Conservative administrations at County Hall authorized substantial

LEFT: Looking west at Acton Town, where the Piccadilly and District lines divide. The approaching 1973 stock train has come on the Piccadilly from Heathrow. Ealing Common District line depot and London Transport Museum's Acton Depot are on the right.

OPPOSITE, ABOVE: The award-winning 'Fly the Tube' poster by FCB Advertising, 1978 (left). London Transport were still using the same slogan for the Heathrow Tube service in 1986 (right). The illustration is by Wilson McLean.

OPPOSITE, BELOW: Heathrow Terminal 4 station by London Transport Architects, 1986: a further move away from the bland design styles of the 1960s and early 1970s.

# Fly the Tube

HEATHROW CENTRAL ⟲

Take the Piccadilly Line to Heathrow Airport.
It's the only way to fly.

**Fly the Tube to Heathrow**

**LEFT, ABOVE:** The Jubilee line platforms at Charing Cross opened in 1979 and closed twenty years later when the Jubilee line extension (JLE) to Stratford was built on a different route avoiding the City and running through Westminster.

**LEFT, BELOW:** A D78 stock car, introduced on the District line in 1980. These trains broke with Underground tradition by having brightly coloured moquette seating in orange, yellow and black, but retained the Canadian maple flooring. The interiors were completely redesigned in the 1990s.

**OPPOSITE:** A Charing Cross Northern line platform, 1979, decorated with wood engravings by David Gentleman, showing the original medieval cross for Queen Eleanor being constructed. The artist's tiny artworks were enlarged and printed on Warerite panels for the full platform length, creating an uninterrupted artwork with no advertising that still looks good.

CHARING CROSS

revenue subsidies to London Transport at this time, but there was no serious planning for the future of the city's transport and certainly no commitment from the politicians about what they were trying to achieve. London Transport itself became a political football, with little vision and weak management.

Horace Cutler, the Conservative leader of the GLC from 1977, castigated the London Transport Board at this time for being 'unable to make up its mind whether it was a commercial undertaking, a social service or a mixture of the two'. In his memoirs, published in 1981, Cutler describes it as 'the largest public transport organization and an albatross round the neck of the capital's ratepayers'. Yet under his brief leadership, the GLC offered no coherent way forward.

The line's name change from 'Fleet' to 'Jubilee' was taken from the Conservative manifesto for the 1977 GLC elections. This was in honour of the Queen's Silver Jubilee year, although perhaps aimed also at easing open government coffers for the next stage of the project. Yet by the time the very short first stage of the Jubilee line was opened by Prince Charles in 1979, the future extension of the line was on hold indefinitely. Few saw much benefit to London in this short diversion by just three stations of one branch of the old Bakerloo, and existing passengers thought the change inconvenient and wasteful.

Rampant inflation and loss of income from road congestion continued to erode London Transport's financial position. In

1975, two fare increases were necessary, well above the rate of inflation. By 1976, fare inflation had risen to 25 per cent while passenger numbers on the Tube dropped by 5 per cent and continued to fall every year until 1982, when they bottomed out at 498 million passenger journeys. This was a huge decline from the peak of 720 million in 1948 on a smaller network. Car ownership in the capital was still increasing by 1 per cent a year, while beyond the bright new Jubilee line the Underground fell into decline. Staff morale was poor, the travelling environment was strewn with litter and cigarette ends, and crime on the system was rising.

A concentration on rolling stock replacement in the 1970s left little money available to improve the Underground traveller's static environment. In fact, hardly any modernization of the predominantly Victorian and Edwardian central area stations took place between 1940 and 1980. Then, in 1981, a systematic approach to station modernization began when the GLC approved a £60-million rolling programme to refurbish about 150 stations, scheduled to continue into the 1990s.

### Fares Fair

Various surveys have indicated that a bright, modern environment helps to encourage passenger numbers and gives travellers an increased sense of security. No doubt the station modernization programme contributed to the rise in passenger

Eduardo Paolozzi's 1984 mosaics, inspired by the local electronics retailers on Tottenham Court Road, were another attempt to give a refurbished Tube station a sense of place. Battered and damaged over the years, the mosaics were re-sited and recreated before the arrival of Crossrail and now gleam anew around the TCR complex.

Way out

Northern line

Way out

numbers on the Underground in the 1980s, but it seems likely that the key factor here was the actual cost of travel, which provoked the great 'Fares Fair' controversy that gripped the capital in 1981.

During the course of 1980, with Cutler's Conservatives in control at County Hall, London Transport fares were increased twice, by nearly 20 per cent and then by more than 13 per cent. Almost inevitably, the cost of travel in London became a key issue in the GLC elections the following year. In May 1981, Labour came to power with a manifesto promise to cut London Transport fares by 25 per cent. The day after the election, the left-wing Ken Livingstone successfully ousted the moderate Andrew McIntosh as Labour leader. It was the first step in what became a fight to the death between Livingstone's municipal socialist GLC and Margaret Thatcher's free-marketeering Conservative government, which had been elected in 1979. London Transport was caught in the crossfire between County Hall and the Palace of Westminster.

On GLC instructions, London Transport introduced the 'Fares Fair' scheme on 4 October 1980; this included a full system of zonal fares throughout the bus and Underground network and an average fare reduction of as much as 32 per cent. Passenger usage of buses and Tubes instantly shot up from 5.5 to 6 million a day, and there was a marked reduction in both car use and traffic congestion.

These benefits were to be financed by an additional £125 million a year on the rates, bringing London's level of public transport subsidy up from 29 per cent to 56 per cent. This was on a par with Paris, but still well below many other cities in Europe and the United States. However, the legality of the GLC's supplementary rate demand was challenged in the courts by Bromley Council, an outer London borough with no Underground service. Bromley won its case against the GLC on appeal, with the Law Lords ruling that under their interpretation of the Transport (London) Act 1969, London Transport must plan, so far as possible, to break even.

The ending of 'Fares Fair' in March 1982 meant a 100 per cent increase to meet the financial remit required by this judgment. Passenger numbers on both the buses and the Underground then plummeted from 6 million to 5 million a day. Eventually, a compromise was reached in May 1983, when fares were cut again by 25 per cent and the zonal fare structure was further simplified. 'Fares Fair' had demonstrated that cheaper fares did indeed attract greater patronage and had excited significant debate about the wider social and economic role of public transport. A second legacy was the simplification of ticketing represented by zonal fares and the introduction of the travelcard. Only the radical shake-up of 'Fares Fair' could have changed the Underground's long-term mindset against zonal ticketing.

## ⭕ New Art on the Tube

A concern for high-quality applied art and design on the Tube had first been introduced and developed by Frank Pick in the 1920s. After lapsing in the 1950s and 1960s, it returned in the 1980s through the station refurbishment programme led by London Transport's architects and through new direct poster commissions from artists and designers after a reliance on advertising agencies in the 1970s. Since 2000, Art on the Underground has developed an extensive programme of temporary and permanent public art commissions for London Underground. These include a variety of art forms and media, located all over the Tube. They range from community projects to Tube map covers, from curated art installations on the disused platform at Gloucester Road to the outside walls of a new electricity sub-station at Edgware Road. In multiple ways, art is now embedded on the Tube and forming an ever-changing part of its unique cultural landscape.

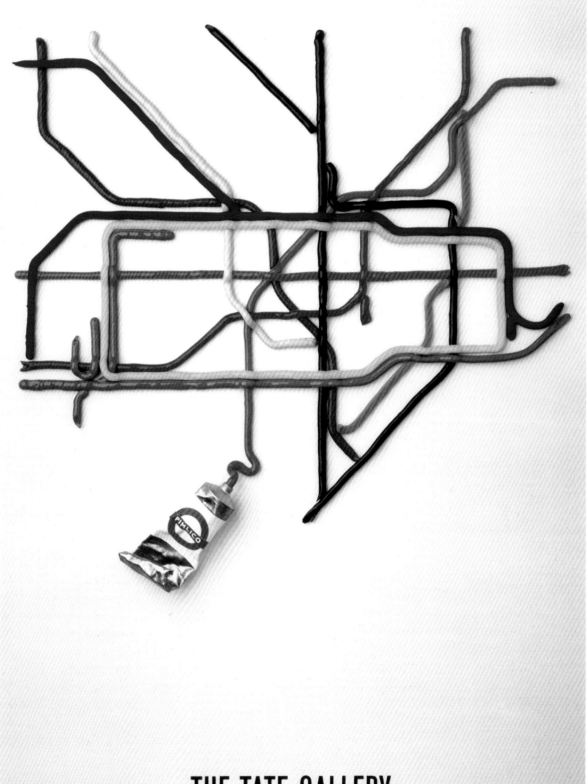

**THE TATE GALLERY**
*by Tube*

One of a series of new paintings commissioned by London Underground

LEFT, ABOVE: Sherlock Holmes-themed tiling at Baker Street (Bakerloo platforms), refurbished by London Transport architects in the 1980s.

LEFT, BELOW: In 2018, *my name is lettie eggysrub* by Heather Phillipson, an installation of outsized eggs, chicken parts and video screens, appeared at Gloucester Road station.

RIGHT: By far the most popular of the new 'Art on the Underground' posters commissioned in the late 1980s was one of the very first, created in 1986. 'Tate Gallery by Tube' was a perfect visual pun, designed by the Fine White Line agency, using a model 'tube' and paint 'lines' to make a 3D Tube map. It was the London Transport Museum shop's best-seller for many years.

The political legacy of 'Fares Fair' was a continuing confrontation between national and London government, which eventually led to the vindictive abolition of the GLC by the Conservative government in 1986. It was a clear political victory for Thatcher at the time, but when the Labour government of 1997 created a new local authority for the capital, Livingstone had the last laugh by returning as the first elected mayor of London. His strong support for public transport improvements was a major factor in his successful election, and as chairman of the new transport authority, Transport for London, Livingstone confirmed that his top priority was 'breaking London's transport logjam'.

In the short term, London Transport was removed from GLC control and a new corporation – London Regional Transport (LRT) – took over. LRT was directly responsible to the Secretary of State for Transport, who set the new authority the almost impossible task of improving London's bus and Underground services while halving the level of revenue support from tax and ratepayers. Two wholly owned subsidiary companies of LRT – London Buses and London Underground – were set up in 1985 to run the bus and Underground networks on the corporation's behalf.

In its first annual report, London Underground was able to announce that more passengers had used the system than ever before. In 1985–6, London Underground carried 762 million passengers, well above its previous record total of 720 million in 1948. At the same time, operating costs were significantly reduced by a new system of train overhaul and the introduction of more driver-only operation. The Underground ticketing system swept away all previous machines and gates, and installed new self-service ticket machines from 1987 onwards at every station, with entry and exit gates in the central area.

Having hit the bottom, the Underground was to benefit from the remarkable and unpredicted turnaround in London's fortunes from the mid-1980s, as the city's population and economy began to grow again. Fuelled by the Big Bang, the deregulation of London's financial markets on 27 October 1986, the Stock Exchange was opened up and transformed. The Big Bang secured the City's status as a global centre for financial services and fostered a turnaround in London's economy, underpinning its renewed world city status – a focus for economic investment, the creative industries, tourism and ultimately the Olympic Games in 2012.

London Transport's return to central government control in 1984 was a nationalization that ran counter to the Thatcher government's policy of privatization for state-owned industries. This was an indication of how bitter her political battle with Livingstone's GLC had become, but it also conceded that London Transport could not be readily privatized. While parts of the great state-owned organization,

such as bus engineering, could be closed down and bus routes put out to tender for private company operation, it was not so easy to carve up the Underground into separate packages.

Tony Ridley, London Underground's managing director, found that by the mid-1980s the key challenge of his job had changed suddenly from a directive to 'stop the decline' into a new question: 'How are we going to cope with this enormous growth in traffic?' The unexpected economic boom posed a different issue: downsizing the Tube was clearly not an option but adapting the engineering-led culture of the Underground to cope with new growth was almost equally difficult. On 18 November 1987, the future of the Tube was determined by a tragic and fatal event that forced the organization in a new direction. This was the terrible escalator fire at King's Cross station, which killed thirty-one people and made a completely new approach to safety management and the operation of the whole system essential.

The Fennell Report published in November 1988, one year after the fire, provided a forensic insight into not only the fire but also the management ethos and organizational culture of London Underground that had allowed it to happen. The immediate cause of the fire was a match discarded by a smoker on an old wooden escalator, which ignited combustible material underneath, but the incident exposed a system of inadequate maintenance, a lack of fire safety training and poor evacuation procedures. The report called for 'a much more searching and outward-looking approach to safety management, which will demand a willingness to embrace new ideas'. It also insisted that the old idea of engineers running a railway must be replaced with a recognition at all levels of the responsibility of providing a safe and secure mass passenger transport service for the public. London Transport had been moving cautiously and incrementally for years towards a complete smoking ban in trains and stations, which was only implemented in full after the tragedy at King's Cross.

Both Ridley and Keith Bright, the chairman of LRT, were obliged to resign when the critical Fennell Report was published. It fell to Denis Tunnicliffe, who had recently been appointed by Ridley as joint managing director after the fire, to implement Fennell's recommendations and tackle the change of culture that the Underground needed. Coming from the aviation industry, Tunnicliffe found that the primacy of safety was second nature. He was also untainted in that he was new to the railway industry and was able to deploy what he later described as 'heroic naivety': 'Why do we need to change it? Because we killed thirty-one people.'

The Fennell Report was more than a wake-up call. It forced London Underground to confront its weaknesses and to work towards creating a system that was more resilient, one that London could rely on. A complete overhaul of the

**OPPOSITE, ABOVE AND RIGHT:**
Three potential 'Tube trains of the future' put into service in 1986 to test public reaction. Nobody was keen on the hard seats, but the external sliding doors seemed to find favour. Both were adopted for the next new train design chosen in the 1990s.

**BELOW:** In the aftermath of the Kings Cross fire there was a complete review of safety and security procedures on the Tube. Specially designed Help Points were fitted to every station platform on the system in the 1990s, putting passengers directly in touch with control rooms.

LEFT: 'The Trains Now Arriving...': Announcing a major programme of train refurbishment in the 1990s with the new corporate livery applied on the outside and complete redesign of train interiors in a rolling programme from 1994. This eventually covered all existing trains on the Circle, Hammersmith & City, Victoria and Bakerloo lines.

OPPOSITE: The Piranesi-like Jubilee line extension (JLE) station at Westminster, built directly below the District and Circle line platforms without interrupting the service.

# The trains now arriving...

We're starting to improve our trains from top to bottom to give you a more pleasant and more comfortable journey.

The first examples, with bright new interiors and eye-catching livery are entering service on the Circle and Hammersmith & City lines.

Victoria and Bakerloo line passengers will see the way ahead this month when their first trains start to arrive.

Our aim is simple. To give London an Underground to be proud of.

# A new dawn for the heart of London.

safety systems and a determined refurbishment and major clean-up of the entire network were undertaken in the 1990s. The Underground had to become, in new managing director Tunnicliffe's phrase, 'a decently modern metro'. The transformation of the entire system in these years, including the care and presentation of every train, station and piece of equipment, was quite remarkable.

### The Jubilee Line Extension

The key development project that spearheaded the Tube's recovery in the 1990s was the Jubilee line extension (JLE). Despite it being delayed and finishing well over budget, it came to be seen eventually as London Underground's greatest achievement at the close of the twentieth century. Having been dismissed as far too expensive in 1980, this new Tube development was to become, twenty years later, the saviour of Canary Wharf.

Stage two of the Jubilee line had effectively been abandoned during the political and financial battles of the early 1980s. At the same time, the early proposals for regenerating London's Docklands were to construct a cheap and cheerful automated light railway rather than an expensive new Tube to provide public transport.

When the initial Docklands Light Railway (DLR) network opened in 1987, it was plagued with failures and problems with the computer control systems, which necessitated major upgrades and the virtual reconstruction of the network. Meanwhile, the Canary Wharf development had grown into a complete financial services district, occupying 1 million square metres (10.7 million sq ft) of the former West India Docks. Canadian developers Olympia & York, owned by the Reichmann brothers who took over the original Canary Wharf scheme, were then the biggest property company in the world. They planned to build a giant business centre, which would create offices and homes for least 50,000 people, in a new Manhattan-on-Thames at the heart of the Isle of Dogs.

This suddenly changed the transport requirements for Docklands. It was clear that even with an upgrade the DLR would be unable to cope with the numbers. The Reichmanns needed a proper railway, which had to be on a bigger scale. The Canary Wharf development depended on transport capacity if investors and tenants were to be convinced to make the seismic move out of the City to Docklands. In 1988, the Reichmanns opened an exhibition of their scheme near Parliament to start lobbying the Thatcher government, which was already a strong advocate and believer in private-sector partnerships providing (and funding) public services. A deal was reached whereby the Reichmanns would contribute one-third of the cost of building a revised JLE to Canary Wharf on a new route.

Canada Water JLE station followed the Underground tradition of incorporating a bus interchange (left) at a major intersection. The bus station is by Eva Jiřičná Architects, the only architectural practice on the JLE project led by a woman.

The fortunes of Canary Wharf and the JLE soon became inextricably linked in a roller coaster of boom and bust in the 1990s. In May 1992, in response to the London commercial property collapse, Olympia & York went into administration and the Canary Wharf development came to an abrupt halt. Having been dragged reluctantly into building the Reichmanns' railway, the Underground now found itself rescuing it.

Canary Wharf Ltd came out of administration in October 1993, releasing £98 million to begin work on the JLE project. The prime minister, John Major, formally initiated construction at the site of Canary Wharf station two months later. The 16 km (10 mile) JLE was to run on a revised route, leaving the 1979 alignment of the Jubilee line at Green Park to go via Westminster, then south of the river via Waterloo and London Bridge, through Docklands and north to Stratford. It would no longer run through the City and the original Charing Cross terminus was set to be abandoned once it became a stub end of the new JLE.

London Underground set out to learn from the Victoria line and the first stage of the Jubilee line project experience, as well as from the King's Cross fire. As London was no longer at the vanguard of international metro development, it looked to the latest developments overseas. London Transport's new chairman from 1988 was Sir Wilfrid Newton, who was recruited from the rapidly growing Mass Transit Railway in Hong Kong,

one of the most advanced and successful modern metros. He brought in Roland Paoletti, chief architect of the Mass Transit Railway, to oversee the design of the JLE. 'Quite an unusual sort of chap,' he told Tunnicliffe, 'but he's very good.'

The new stations were made as spacious as possible below ground, sitting in massive concrete boxes. In contrast to the penny-pinching Victoria line, new features included step-free access from street to train, dual exits at both ends of station platforms for safe evacuation, smoke ventilation systems, platform-edge doors, fireproof lifts and at least three escalators at each station. Paoletti did not design the structures himself but commissioned several external architectural practices to work with his team on each of the eleven new stations and the Stratford Market train depot.

It was quite different from the Pick/Holden approach, but the result was creative variety and quality architecture within a very strong and coherent overall design vision, bringing architects and engineers together at every level. 'Even Holden didn't get below ground,' remarked Paoletti; 'the architecture ran out in the ticket hall.'

Without question, the JLE represents some of the finest modern public design in late twentieth-century London, although when it opened in 1999 its legacy was obscured by cost over-runs and delays. The most serious problem was the failure to introduce automatic train operation and the

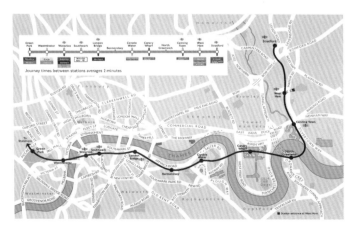

LEFT, ABOVE: Westminster platform, 1999, showing the safety screen and doors adopted at all new JLE stations in the wake of the King's Cross fire.

LEFT, BELOW: The JLE route map. The line opened just in time for the Millennium on 31 December 1999, but was well over budget and without the new moving block signalling, which arrived twelve years late.

OPPOSITE, ABOVE: Southwark JLE station entrance, with TfL's Palestra office building opposite.

OPPOSITE, BELOW: The impressive high-tech platform-level concourse at Southwark, designed by Sir Richard MacCormac, 1999.

# Docklands Light Railway

London's inner docks began to close in the 1960s because they could not handle the large ships used for container traffic. When plans were considered to redevelop the derelict former docklands of east London, it was realized that a new public transport system was essential to encourage both commercial and residential regeneration. The Isle of Dogs was particularly isolated, with no rail links to the rest of London and few local bus routes. The original intention, in the 1970s, had been to continue the Jubilee line eastwards as a link with central London, but in 1981 the government set up the London Docklands Development Corporation to explore cheaper alternatives that would encourage regeneration. Light rail – as opposed to an express bus, guided bus or conventional Underground system – was recommended as the most cost-effective transport solution.

In 1982, construction of the Docklands Light Railway (DLR) was authorized. It was designed as a stand-alone rapid transit system to provide a low-cost link between the Isle of Dogs, where a new business hub was planned at Canary Wharf, and London's existing financial centre in the City, together with wider areas of east London. By reusing the trackbed of some derelict freight lines linked together by new elevated sections featuring tight curves and steep gradients, the DLR would be the updated equivalent of a conventional tramway, although without any street running. It would use articulated passenger cars based on the modern trams that ran in German cities, but with no drivers. The latest computer technology would allow remote, fully automated train control, and as the DLR would be off-street it could use third-rail power pick-up instead of overhead wires. A complete initial network was built very quickly, in just two years, all within a tight budget of £77 million. It was ready for a royal opening by the Queen in 1987.

The construction of the DLR occurred at a time when the estimated cost of a Tube extension to Docklands was £325 million. However, the cost savings and apparent cheapness of the DLR soon proved to be short lived and largely illusory. In its early years, the DLR got a regular pasting in the London *Evening Standard* as an unreliable 'Mickey Mouse' system, unable to cope with the growing number of commuters travelling to Docklands as Canary Wharf developed. Expensive reconstruction and upgrading of the control systems, extensions to the Bank and into south and east London, with better connections and new, longer trains, were all necessary in the 1990s.

After an initial bumpy ride, the DLR became, in the early twenty-first century, one of the fastest growing and most reliable rail systems in the country. It now comprises six branches, covering 38 km (24 miles) of track, with forty-five stations and 120 million passengers a year. It is not part of the Underground, but the DLR now comes under the London Rail division of TfL and is currently operated under a franchise awarded by TfL to KeolisAmey Docklands, a joint venture between transport operator Keolis and infrastructure specialists Amey.

BELOW: 'Catching the Light': one of the first DLR posters issued soon after the system opened in 1987, but before the main Canary Wharf development had taken off.

BOTTOM: The DLR in 2018, showing the elevated structure and tight curves used on most sections of the railway.

Stratford station, which has grown considerably since the JLE's arrival in 1999, now also serves the DLR, Overground and a major bus station, as well as the Central line and suburban services from Liverpool Street, making it the main transport interchange in east London. It came into its own at the London Olympics in 2012.

new 'moving block' signalling system to enable closer train headways. This took another twelve years to achieve, with regular failures and weekend closures during the lengthy upgrade. Now the JLE can run up to thirty-three trains per hour; it soaks up passengers at peak times and has been key to the further regeneration of Docklands and east London, including the success of the Olympics and Paralympics in 2012.

## Transport for London

The Labour government of Tony Blair, elected in 1997, kept a manifesto promise to set up a new city-wide local authority for London to replace the GLC, which had been dissolved in 1986. It was to be led by an elected mayor, whose biggest financial responsibility would be transport, including London Underground. Transport for London (TfL), a new organization created in 2000, replaced London Transport but took on much wider responsibilities, including taxis, river services, the DLR, Croydon Tramlink, cycling and streets as well as bus services and the Tube.

A sticking point in carrying out the transfer to TfL was the proposed funding mechanism for the continued maintenance and modernization of the Underground. The government had decided to set up a Public–Private Partnership to do this, committing TfL as the public authority to thirty-year contracts with private consortia, who would be paid to carry out the

agreed upgrade work. The first mayor of London, Livingstone, was elected on an independent ticket and would not agree to carry through the New Labour policy on this, which he believed suggested a preference for private management of the public realm, similar to Thatcher's approach. After fighting it in the courts, Livingstone was forced to accept a complex and flawed method of funding for the Tube that nobody fully understood.

Contracts were signed with two newly created infrastructure companies (Metronet and Tube Lines) in 2003, but by 2007 Metronet had collapsed and in 2010 Tube Lines was dissolved, with all work returning to in-house management. As a means of financing the Tube's ongoing costs, the Public–Private Partnership was abandoned and quietly paid off, an embarrassing and very expensive failure. London Underground is now an integrated public company again, part of TfL and responsible to the London mayor at City Hall, not the government at Westminster.

Despite this clash over the Public–Private Partnership, there has been a far more strategic approach to transport planning in London since the creation of TfL and mayoral governance. The Underground remained resilient through the trauma of the 7/7 suicide bomb attacks of 2005 and the excitement of the London Olympics in 2012. Despite the financial crash of 2008 and the onset of recession, passenger numbers on the Tube reached record levels, with more than 1.2 billion annual journeys. Most

The escalators to the main JLE hall at Canary Wharf, 1999. The station was designed by Sir Norman Foster and occupies a former ship dock, enabling it to cope with much larger crowds than any other London Tube station.

of these are now made using cashless payments, which have grown dramatically since the introduction of the original Oyster smartcard in 2003, which revolutionized payment and ticketing across all travel modes in the city.

## Overground and Crossrail

The creation of TfL in 2000 and mayoral governance led to a far more strategic approach to transport planning in the city than was ever possible under London Transport. Two major twenty-first-century rail development projects linked to the Underground, but not actually part of it, demonstrate this improvement. They both help meet new travel needs and increase capacity on London's public transport, which are the main concerns of planners and passengers in an increasingly global city.

London Overground was created by TfL in 2007 to manage a number of suburban rail services transferred from the national network. Some had been run down and neglected for many years as part of British Rail. For the first time since the nineteenth century, the benefits of running orbital passenger services around London's inner suburbs, linked to radial routes through the centre, was recognized. By reinstating and upgrading old routes and creating new links at both ends of the fully refurbished and extended East London line, a complete orbital metro network was created and opened in stages

between 2010 and 2012. It runs through twenty of London's thirty-three boroughs, and 30 per cent of Londoners now live less than fifteen minutes' walk from an Overground station.

London Overground has a fleet of new walk-through trains and much-improved services, with a similar but distinct branding to the Underground. In effect, this has put large areas of London that have never had an Underground station – such as Hackney, Peckham and Sydenham – 'on the Tube'. It has also made journeys across and around London's inner suburbs quick and simple, where once they were slow and involved changes as well as going through the centre. The Overground services were so popular and well used that it was decided to order a fifth carriage for each four-car train straight away.

All of the former Network Rail stations on the Overground have been refurbished and rebranded by TfL, just as London Transport did to the London North Eastern Railway surface stations taken over for the Northern and Central line extensions in the 1940s. Where completely new stations have been built, such as Hoxton and Haggerston, these have the quality of the best modern urban design but also make a gesture back to Holden's classic Tube stations of the 1930s.

Crossrail, a far more ambitious project, is a joint venture between TfL and the Department for Transport, to build a new railway right under London, linking Heathrow and Reading in the west with Shenfield and Abbey Wood in the east. New

OPPOSITE: The nearly complete
Tottenham Court Road Crossrail
station in April 2019.

ABOVE: Class 378 Overground trains
introduced in 2009.

RIGHT AND BELOW: The new
Overground station at Haggerston
opened in 2009, designed by
Acanthus LW architects. The
tiled mural in the booking hall by
Tod Hanson commemorates the
seventeenth-century astronomer
and mathematician Edmond Halley,
the first person to calculate the
orbit of a comet, who lived locally.

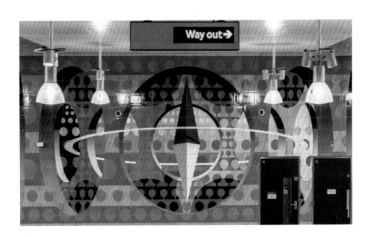

tunnels will take high-frequency main-line-size trains deep below central London, with Tube interchanges at seven new stations between Paddington and Canary Wharf. It is the London equivalent of the Paris RER lines built in the 1970s, which are separate from the city's Métro but linked to it.

Like so many London rail projects, the equivalent of Crossrail was first suggested in the optimistic post-war planning days of the 1940s, but no practical work was done. The name 'Crossrail' emerged in the 1974 London Rail Study Report, which costed an east–west main line under London at an estimated £885 million, but the idea was not pursued. The current project only formally came about in 2001 through Cross London Rail Links, a joint venture between the newly created TfL and the Department for Transport, which is also promoting a new Wimbledon–Hackney scheme that could become Crossrail 2.

The Crossrail Act of 2008 was given royal assent in July 2008, granting Cross London Rail Links the powers necessary to build the line. Construction began on 15 May 2009, and in September 2009 the project received £1 billion in funding, lent to TfL by the European Investment Bank. Both the Labour and Conservative parties made commitments to deliver the railway in their manifestos for the 2010 election, and the coalition government formed after the election also committed to the project. Unlike the controversial High Speed 2 project, Crossrail has met with relatively little opposition and not caused political or wider popular controversy despite the scale of the construction under London.

In fact, the promotion and publicity around the line's construction have been exemplary. It includes a three-part BBC documentary titled *The Fifteen Billion Pound Railway*, made between 2014 and 2018, which covers everything from archaeological revelations in plague pits to the 'urban heart surgery' of precision tunnelling under delicate listed buildings in Soho. The film presents the biggest engineering project in Europe as a race against time, but also, of course, as a human and technological challenge 'from digging out 42 km (26 miles) of tunnels to constructing ten vast new stations'.

All was apparently on budget and on schedule for a royal inauguration in December 2018, when the Queen would open and rename Crossrail the Elizabeth line. In July 2018, the railway was 93 per cent complete and estimated to have cost £15.4 billion. Its main features, the 21 km (13 miles) of twin tunnels below the city, were ready. The new trains had been delivered and were being tested on the overground sections. Suddenly, in August 2018, it was announced that the opening of the core line would be delayed by at least a year. In December, Crossrail announced that further funding was required to finish remaining works and that completion and opening may be further postponed until early 2021.

OPPOSITE: Cross-section of the Canary Wharf Crossrail station, predating the design of the new trains.

LEFT: All-new class 345 Crossrail trains, designed by Bombardier and built in Derby, were delivered in 2018 and available for surface running before tunnel operation was possible.

BELOW: The new Elizabeth line section of Canary Wharf station, known as Crossrail Place.

This is a highly complex project and although it is not yet obvious which aspects of it have gone wrong and caused the delays, it is clearly a combination of factors. Crossrail was almost too high profile, and there should have been more transparency at an earlier stage about the elements of risk. It will have an inevitable knock-on effect on other new capital projects because the loss of at least a year's revenue income from Crossrail will delay other schemes.

London is still growing rapidly. It is estimated that by 2031 there will be an additional 1.8 million people living and working in the capital. That's an extra Tube train of people every three days. As a result, demand for TfL rail services – Underground, Overground, DLR and trams – is growing too, and Crossrail alone will not increase the system capacity enough.

TfL started planning for this in 2014 with a comprehensive New Tube for London strategy to upgrade the existing areas of the deep Tube that have not been modernized in the twenty-first century. The plan is to replace existing signalling and train control systems, including power and track enhancements. A new standard design of articulated, walk-through trains will improve capacity, frequency and the major problem of the Tube's tight environment where air cooling in the smaller trains and deep stations has proved extremely challenging. The first line to be enhanced and equipped with

new trains will be the Piccadilly, currently the busiest, by 2025. Putting definite dates against future developments is already proving unwise, but London Underground and its associated partners under the TfL umbrella are now moving forward with new confidence. Anyone who remembers the grim state of the Tube in the 1980s will recognise the improvements that have been achieved and the progress now being made.

The first twenty-first-century addition to the deep Tube, a short branch off the Northern line at Kennington running under Nine Elms to Battersea, is nearing completion. This will serve the rapidly developing new district of offices and homes around the former power station. A southern extension of the Bakerloo line below the Old Kent Road to Peckham is proposed but not yet under way. Both of these are about improving connectivity and capacity on the Tube but depend on new finance being available. Comprehensive station redevelopments at key pinch points such as Camden Town and South Kensington are still on the wish list.

Whatever the sequence of development, London's Underground will be ever more vital to the future of the city. The Tube will remain, in Frank Pick's phrase, the 'framework of the town' and there is a strong possibility that TfL may yet become responsible for a rail network over an even wider area, an integrated metro for London and the south-east.

OPPOSITE: Crossrail tunnel test run in 2018.

BELOW: The New Tube for London project includes the next generation of fully automated Tube trains, a single design for use with new signalling and control systems on the Piccadilly, Bakerloo, Central and Waterloo & City lines. The trains have been designed by PriestmanGoode and will be built by Siemens. They will be articulated, walk-through units to maximize passenger space, and subject to the installation of new signalling and control systems should enter service initially on the Piccadilly line by 2025.

RIGHT, ABOVE: Helen, one of the two giant Tunnel Boring Machines (TBMs) used on the Battersea extension of the Northern line, being installed in 2017. The TBM was named after Helen Sharman, the first British woman astronaut. Tunnelling was completed in 2018, but the new line will not open until 2021.

RIGHT, MIDDLE: Crossrail engineers in front of a tunnel boring machine (TBM) after breakthrough.

LONDON 2026 A.D.—THIS IS ALL IN TH

TO-DAY — THE SOLID COMFORT OF THE UNDE

'London 2026 AD: This is All in the Air' – poster by Montagu Black, 1926. This view envisages a London of skyscrapers and autogyros but still with an Underground. The year 2026 is also the date envisaged for the arrival of HS2.

TfL rail services map, 2019. In addition to the eleven lines of London Underground, these include the DLR, London Trams and London Overground services. By 2021 it will also include the Elizabeth line and the Northern line branch extension from Kennington to Battersea Power Station.

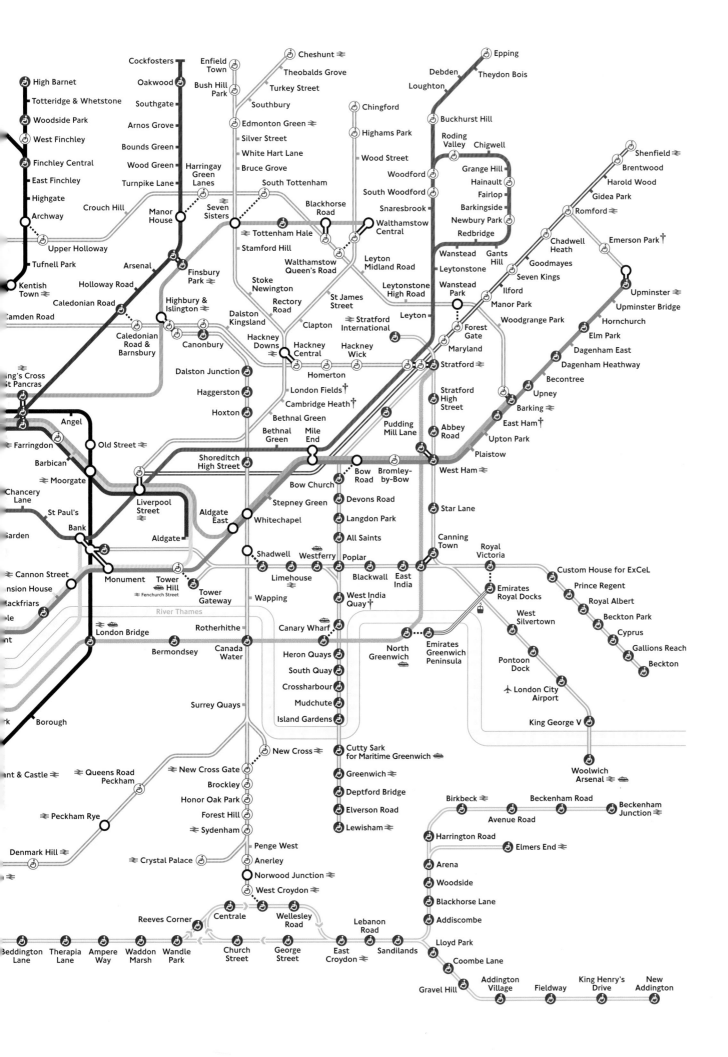

# Timeline

**1863** Metropolitan Railway opens the first passenger-carrying underground railway in the world between Paddington (Bishop's Road) and Farringdon Street (now part of the Circle line).

**1868** Metropolitan District Railway opens between South Kensington and Westminster (now part of the District and Circle lines).

**1869** East London Railway starts running steam trains through the Thames Tunnel, built under the river between Rotherhithe and Wapping by Marc Brunel. It had opened as a foot tunnel in 1843 (now part of the London Overground).

**1870** Tower Subway opens under the river near the Tower of London, the first Tube tunnel built using a shield.

**1880** Metropolitan Railway 'Extension line' running north-west out of London from Baker Street reaches Harrow-on-the-Hill.

**1884** Completion of the Inner Circle (now part of the Circle line) by linking up the Metropolitan and District lines at both ends. It is then jointly operated by the two original underground companies.

**1890** City & South London Railway opens the world's first deep-level electric Tube railway between Stockwell and King William Street (now part of the Northern line).

**1898** Waterloo & City Railway opens.

**1900** Central London Railway ('Twopenny Tube') opens between Shepherd's Bush and Bank (now part of the Central line).

**1902** Creation of the Underground Electric Railways of London (UERL) Ltd, a holding company known as the Underground Group.

**1904** Great Northern & City Railway opens between Finsbury Park and Moorgate (now part of Network Rail). Metropolitan Railway branch from Harrow to Uxbridge opens.

**1905** The District, Circle and part of the Metropolitan Railway are electrified.

**1906** Baker Street & Waterloo Railway opens between Baker Street and Elephant & Castle (part of what is now the Bakerloo line). Great Northern, Piccadilly & Brompton Railway opens between Finsbury Park and Hammersmith (now part of the Piccadilly line).

**1907** Charing Cross, Euston & Hampstead Railway opens from Charing Cross to Golders Green and Highgate (Archway) (now part of the Northern line). Albert Stanley becomes general manager of the UERL.

**1908** Start of co-ordinated marketing and branding across the separate underground railway companies, promoted by Frank Pick. The first version of the bar-and-disc symbol is introduced on Tube station platforms.

**1911** First escalator on the Tube is installed at Earl's Court.

**1912–13** UERL takes over two independent Tube lines (Central London and C&SLR) and the main bus company (LGOC) and becomes known as the Combine. Metropolitan Railway takes over the Great Northern & City Tube and acquires the East London Railway, which it electrifies.

**1914–18** First World War.

**1915–16** Women first employed extensively by UERL and Metropolitan Railway as 'wartime substitutes'.

**1916** Edward Johnston completes the first design of his classic sans serif letterface for Underground signage and posters.

**1917** Bakerloo line services extended to Watford Junction (now London Overground services beyond Harrow & Wealdstone).

**1924–6** Underground extensions north to Edgware and south to Morden, combined with reconstruction and link to the City & South London Railway completed (all now part of the Northern line).

**1928** Reconstruction of Piccadilly Circus completed, the Underground's showpiece station in the heart of London.

**1929** New London Underground headquarters open at 55 Broadway, designed by Charles Holden.

**1932–3** Piccadilly line extensions open north of Finsbury Park to Cockfosters and west of Hammersmith, including Holden's finest modern station designs. Metropolitan Railway branch opens from Wembley Park to Stanmore (now part of the Jubilee line).

**1933** First printing of Harry Beck's iconic Underground diagram. The London Passenger Transport Board (LPTB) is created as a single public corporation to run all bus, tram and underground railway services in London. The new body is soon known simply as London Transport.

**1935–40** New Works Programme includes a new Bakerloo line extension from Baker Street to Stanmore (part of the Jubilee line since 1979) and Northern line extension beyond Archway to link up with and electrify the LNER's surface branch lines at East Finchley.

**1938** Introduction of 1938 stock, the classic London Tube train, by W.S. Graff-Baker.

**1939–45** Second World War. Thousands of Londoners take shelter in Tube stations during wartime bombing raids.

**1946–9** Opening of Central line extensions east and west, begun in the 1930s but suspended during the war.

**1948** London Transport is nationalized as the London Transport Executive.

**1952** First unpainted silver aluminium alloy train introduced on the District line.

**1961** Electrification of Metropolitan line from Rickmansworth to Amersham and Chesham, ending use of steam and electric locomotives on London Transport passenger trains.

**1963** London Transport Executive becomes the London Transport Board, reporting directly to the Minister for Transport.

**1968–9** Victoria line opens between Walthamstow Central and Victoria, with automatic trains and ticket gates.

**1970** London Transport is transferred to Greater London Council (GLC) control.

**1971** Victoria line extension opens to Brixton.

**1977** First airport link for the Tube as Piccadilly extension from Hounslow West opens to Heathrow.

**1978** First woman driver on the London Underground, Hannah Dadds, starts work on the District line.

**1979** First stage of Jubilee line opens between Charing Cross and Baker Street.

**1983** Introduction of zonal fares and the Travelcard on the Underground.

**1984** Government removes London Transport from GLC control, renaming it London Regional Transport (LRT), reporting directly to the Secretary of State for Transport.

**1985** London Underground Ltd formed as a subsidiary company of LRT but still in public ownership. The Tube is underfunded and in decline.

**1987** Docklands Light Railway (DLR) opens. A serious escalator fire at King's Cross Underground station kills thirty-one people. An extensive clean-up, modernization and the introduction of new safety standards across the network follow this tragedy in the 1990s.

**1999** Jubilee line extension (JLE) opens from Green Park to Stratford.

**2000** Transport for London created as a new overall transport authority for the capital.

**2002–3** Public–Private Partnership (PPP) contracts drawn up for maintenance and upgrading of all Underground lines on behalf of LU. The Oyster card cashless touch-ticketing system is introduced.

**2003–4** LU signs PPP contracts with Tubelines and Metronet.

**2005** 7/7 coordinated suicide bomb attacks on three Underground trains and a bus kill fifty-two people.

**2007** London Overground is created as part of TfL to upgrade and manage some suburban rail services. East London line closes for rebuilding, extension and transfer from LU to London Overground management. London Underground carries one billion passengers in a year for the first time.

**2009** Start of Crossrail construction.

**2010** S stock is introduced on the Metropolitan line.

**2010–12** Completion of orbital rail links all round London as part of the growing London Overground network.

**2013** London Underground 150th anniversary celebrations including a steam run over the original section of the Metropolitan Railway.

**2016** Start of Night Tube services.

**2020** Opening of Crossrail, now renamed the Elizabeth line.

**2021** Opening of the Northern line branch extension to Battersea Power Station.

# Index

# Index

# Further Reading

Badsey-Ellis, Anthony *The Hampstead Tube: A History of the First 100 Years* (Capital Transport 2007)

Barker, T.C. and Robbins, Michael *A History of London Transport Vols 1 and 2* (Allen & Unwin 1963 and 1974)

Bownes, David and Green, Oliver (eds) *London Transport Posters* (Lund Humphries 2008)

Bownes, David, Green, Oliver and Mullins, Sam *Underground: How the Tube Shaped London* (Allen Lane 2012)

Connor, J.E. *London's Disused Underground Stations* (Capital Transport 2001)

Connor, Piers *The London Underground Electric Train* (The Crowood Press 2015)

Croome, Desmond F. and Jackson, Alan A. *Rails Through the Clay: A History of London's Tube Railways* (Capital Transport, 1993)

Dillon, Tamsin (ed.) *Platform for Art: Art on the Underground* (Black Dog Publishing 2007)

Dobbin, Claire *London Underground Maps: Art, Design and Cartography* (Lund Humphries/London Transport Museum 2012)

Glover, John *London's Overground* (Ian Allan 2011)

Green, Oliver *Frank Pick's London: Art, Design and the Modern City* (V&A Publishing/London Transport Museum 2013)

Green, Oliver *The Tube: Station to Station on the London Underground* (Shire Books 2010)

Green, Oliver and Rewse-Davies, Jeremy *Designed for London: 150 Years of Transport Design* (Laurence King, 1995)

Gregg, John *The Shelter of the Tubes: Tube Sheltering in Wartime London* (Capital Transport, 2001)

Halliday, Stephen *Underground to Everywhere: London's Underground Railway in the Life of the Capital* (Sutton Publishing, 2001)

Horne, Mike *The Piccadilly Tube: A History of the First 100 Years* (Capital Transport, 2007)

Horne, Mike *London's District Railway Vol. 1: The Nineteenth Century* (Capital Transport 2018)

Jackson, Alan A. *London's Metropolitan Railway* (David & Charles 1986)

Jackson, Alan A. *London's Metro-land: A Unique British Railway Enterprise* (Capital Transport 2006)

Lawrence, David *Underground Architecture* (Capital Transport 1994)

Martin, Andrew *Underground, Overground: A Passenger's History of the Tube* (Profile Books, 2013)

Moss, Paul *Underground Movement* (Capital Transport 2000)

Ovenden, Mark *London Underground by Design* (Penguin Books 2013)

Powell, Kenneth *The Jubilee Line Extension* (Laurence King 2000)

Pritchard, Robert and Yearsley, Alan *UK Metro and Light Rail Systems* (Platform 5 Publishing 2017)

Wolmar, Christian *The Subterranean Railway: How the London Underground Was Built and How It Changed the City Forever* (Atlantic Books 2004)

Wolmar, Christian *The Story of Crossrail* (Head of Zeus Publishing 2018)

First published in 2019 by White Lion Publishing,
an imprint of The Quarto Group.
The Old Brewery, 6 Blundell Street
London, N7 9BH,
United Kingdom
T (0)20 7700 6700  F (0)20 7700 8066
www.QuartoKnows.com

A catalogue record for this book is available
from the British Library.

ISBN 978-07112-4013-1

10 9 8 7 6 5 4 3

Typeset in New Johnston
Endpapers by Giovanni Rodolfi

Publisher Jessica Axe
Commissioning editor Melissa Hookway
Editor Cerys Hughes
Project editor Michael Brunström
Designer Glenn Howard

Printed in China

MIX
Paper from
responsible sources
FSC® C124385

## Picture acknowledgments

The author and photographer would like to thank
the staff at London Transport Museum, Transport
for London and London Underground, who
facilitated the new photography and assisted
in the provision of archive images.

All images in this book are © TfL with the
following exceptions.

l=left, r=right, a=above, b=below, m=middle

Alessandro Rota/Getty 201bl
Benjamin Graham 2, 4, 7, 8–9, 10–11, 16b, 18–19,
23b, 24–5, 26a, 27l, 28b, 29br, 31a+b, 32–3, 34a,
37br, 38a+b, 42–3, 44, 50–51, 53, 55a+b, 56a+b,
62a+b, 63b, 64–5, 70–71, 72, 74, 77l+bl, 81r, 82–3,
84a+b, 85r, 87ar+bl, 88l+ar+br, 89, 96–7, 98l, 99,
100, 102–03, 107b, 108b, 112, 114–15, 119, 120,
122l+r, 124–5, 133a+b, 134–5, 138–9, 141r, 142–3,
145, 147ar, 148, 150–51, 155, 158–9, 160a+b, 161,
166a+bl+br, 167, 168–9, 170, 171, 173l+r, 176,
178–9, 184, 188–9, 190l, 198b, 199l+r, 202–3,
204b, 205r, 207a+b, 208–9, 219, 220–21, 229ar,
230–31, 234, 238–9, 240a+b, 244, 247, 248–9, 250a,
251a+b, 252b, 253, 254–5, 257a+bl+br, 259l, 261m
Christian Mueller/Shutterstock 49
Crossrail 256, 258, 259r, 260
EQ Roy/Shutterstock 201br
Photocritical/Shutterstock 245bl
Pictorial Press Ltd/Alamy Stock Photo 15b
The Picture Studio/Shutterstock 61
Popperfoto/Getty 183a
Transport for London and PriestmanGoode 261b
Yale Center for British Art, Paul Mellon Collection
12

Every effort has been made to provide correct
attributions. Any inadvertent errors or omissions
will be corrected in subsequent editions of
this book.

⊖ TFL OFFICIAL LICENSED PRODUCT